BARBEL & CHUB
FISHING

BEING A PRACTICAL TREATISE ON ANGLING WITH FLOAT AND LEDGER IN STILL WATER AND STREAM

INCLUDING A FEW REMARKS ON SURFACE FISHING FOR CHUB

By J.W. MARTIN

THE 'TRENT OTTER'

A Working Man Angler's Experiences; written expressly for the benefit of his brethren of the Craft.

PUBLISHED BY
THE MEDLAR PRESS LIMITED, ELLESMERE
2013

Published by the Medlar Press Limited
The Grange, Ellesmere, Shropshire.
www.medlarpress.com

ISBN 978-1-907110-43-6

First published by J.W.Martin 1896

Designed and typeset in 10½ on 12½ pt Bembo Roman.
Produced in England by The Medlar Press Limited, Ellesmere.
Printed and bound in Great Britain by TJ International, Padstow.

PREFATORY NOTE

My dear brother fishermen, - I have a favour to ask at your hands, and that is; kindly look through this preface, before proceeding to dip into the various chapters that follow. I have a few words specially for your own ears; I also have something to say about myself, and why? I - a humble working-man bottom fisherman, dares to thrust this little effort of my pen, under your noses for favourable consideration.

We may call this preface, nothing more nor less, than taking a few preliminary swims, down a likely looking stream, on the off-chance of getting a bite; and eventually landing a good bag of mixed fish. There are in scores of big towns and cities, thousands of factory and other workers, who dearly love a day's fishing. The workshop bell or steam buzzer at noon on Saturdays, signals a cessation of the week's toil, and soon after troops of these workers are wending their way, rod in hand and basket on back, to the nearest river, drain, canal, or reservoir. The great majority of these working-men anglers are, pure and simple, bottom fishermen; they cannot go to the Trout stream or the Salmon casts, because the expense is too great. They are content to sit quietly on the banks of the humbler waters, watching the float and drinking down a supply of fresh air that renews their strength and fits them for the next week's toil. They consider themselves well rewarded if they only succeed in catching a dish of humble roach, a brace or two of sporting chub, a lively barbel, or slimy bream. Many of these men have not the time to make a complete study of the craft, and reason out for themselves the why and the wherefore of every little detail of fish life and the peculiarities of the finny tribe. There are, I am aware, in every town, working-men anglers who are amazingly clever with the rod; no words of mine would profit them in the least. I have nothing to say to them except 'Go on, my friends, and prosper; and may your lines be cast in pleasant places.' On the other hand, the younger anglers and the novices far outnumber the expert ones. It is to the former that I am now addressing myself, and trust that they will derive some benefit from the instructions here laid down. I find from a practical knowledge of the subject, that the fish principally sought after by the majority of these men, are Barbel, Chub, Roach, and Bream, and the first two of these are treated of in the following pages.

I have divided the book into two separate parts, making each one complete in itself: - 1st, Barbel; and 2nd, Chub; giving details of the outfits, the tackle, the ground-baits, and the hook baits, each one separate and distinct from the others. I also most carefully note the difference between stream fishing and still water fishing, giving the proper seasons of the year in which to use certain baits, and also the state of the water, when it is proper to try them. I had an idea that if these fish were treated at length from a working-man's point of view, the remarks would be gladly welcomed by my fellow working-men. Six out of every ten do not care for the scientific aspect of the affair; they want to know more about the capture of the fish, than what class they would occupy in a naturalist's museum.

In the second place, the pocket of the working-man angler has been constantly before me; he has not much money to buy an expensive outfit, nor yet for every fresh fad or fancy, that are being constantly brought out to wheedle his hard-earned cash from his pockets. The principles I lay down are those of economy, based upon a practical knowledge and experience, extending through many years, and under peculiar advantages. I have not the least hesitation in saying, that a careful study of this part of my subject will be a saving to the angler of many shillings during a single season.

In the third place, I am one of yourselves. For many years I worked, as boy and man, in the fields, the factory, and the workshop, and close to such well known rivers as the Witham, the Trent, the Bedfordshire Ouse, and various other streams and broads in different counties, and have had opportunities of fishing in the company of some of the most expert anglers on those rivers. My trade as a fishing rod maker, has also brought me in contact and communication with fresh-water fishermen from the four quarters of the kingdom. These are great advantages, and have enabled me to study the craft from many and various standpoints.

And lastly, I would ask the critic to be as merciful as he can, remembering the fact that I left school at the early age of ten; and what little I know in the shape of learning has been gleaned and picked up from the wayside and hedges. I will say no more by way of apology except, all that is good in this volume I dedicate to my fellow working men bottom fishers, and commit it into their hands with the greatest confidence.

I shall deal with the Bream and Roach in another volume.

JOHN WM. MARTIN
'The Trent Otter'
November, 1896

CONTENTS

Part I - The Barbel

Part II - The Chub

PART I

THE BARBEL

CHAPTER I

CHARACTERISTICS OF THE BARBEL

Its strength and endurance - Ancient v. Modern Barbel Tackle - Big bags - Its natural history - Weight of Barbel - Its habits and haunts - Barbel as food.

'And the whisker'd barbel pays
His coarser bulk to swell your praise.'

Michael Drayton, the poet, writing some three hundred years ago, said of this well-known denizen of the Trent:- 'The barbel, than which fish a braver doth not swim,' and that writer was either an angler himself, or else he was the friend and companion of an angler, for the line just quoted is an accurate description of the fish in question. For bravery, he is a gem of the first water, and will fight it out with you to the very last gasp. He is very active, powerful, and vigorous, and is just the chap to try the angler's skill, and the strength of his tackle. Did not Dame Juliana Berners, who wrote the first book on angling that ever was penned, say of him, 'The barbel is an evil fysshe to take, for he is so strongly enarmyd in the mouth that there may no weake harnesse (meaning tackle) holde him.' Izaak Walton, too, says, 'He is so strong that he will often break both rod and line if he proves to be a big one.' An old friend once made me a present of 'Buckland's Familiar History of British

Fishes,' and in the pages of that very delightful work I came across a rather extraordinary statement; it was this: 'When a barbel is hooked he always endeavours to strike at the line with his tail to break it.' A barbel is generally hooked at the bottom of the river, and it is impossible to say with any degree of certainty what he does under the circumstances. I never yet have had a chance to see the tactics a barbel adopts when first hooked; but I should say he is more likely to try to ram his old snout under a stone, or drive it into the sand, so I am afraid we shall have to take Buckland's statement with a grain of salt. There is, however, one thing certain about Mr. Barbel: his strength is amazing. His dogged downward boring, and his tremendous rushes, together with his pluck and tenacity of life, prolong the contest far beyond the measure of any other fish of equal weight, the lordly salmon himself not excepted. Did any of my young friends who may be reading this chapter ever hook a four-pound barbel on light tackle, when fishing for roach? If you did, and kept cool, and played him carefully and properly, you may perhaps remember what a job you had, and what a long time it took before you could get on terms with him. But if you lost your presence of mind, and attempted any rude measures, you probably remember how quickly he walked off with part of your tackle, without so much as a 'Thank you.' And another thing I have noticed: a barbel, more than any other fish I am acquainted with, seems to fight shy of the landing net. You perhaps have had a long and desperate struggle with a big one, and he appears to be played out, utterly and thoroughly; he lies exhausted on his back or side, and allows himself to be drawn towards the boat or bank, but no sooner does he catch sight of the landing net than he wakes up suddenly and makes a desperate bolt - very often to his own satisfaction and the angler's discomfiture. And if one is hooked foul, the play he can give is something wonderful. I remember once on the Trent hooking a six-pounder firmly in the root of the tail, and for a time I was like a well-known sporting journalist - I really thought it must have been the 'Jabberwock' himself that I had got hold of; and to mend the matter he was in rushing waters at the foot of the weirs, close to the bottom locks at Newark-on-Trent. Patience, and a good running reel and line at length claimed the victory; but I have an idea that it was the longest, and one of the strongest, tussles I ever had with a fresh-water fish. This being, then, the pluck and strength of barbel, I have no hesitation in saying that if the angler does happen once in a way to get them well on the feed, it is one of the most exciting and enjoyable forms of sport that can possibly be imagined. Some would-be anglers on reading this may say. 'We shall want some very strong and powerful tackle to successfully cope with this fellow,' but don't make a mistake. I am going to show before I have done that the tackle that will kill the chub will, in skilful hands, kill the barbel, and as the fish have become more and more educated the angler's chance of success is all the greater if he fishes with lines and tackle as fine as he dare use. Years ago, in fact, more years than I care to count up, when I was first initiated into the mysteries of barbel fishing, those fish seemed to be less educated than now. They also appeared to be more plentiful. Mind, I only say appeared, there may be as many of them in the river as ever there were; at any rate it was then a good deal easier job to make a bag than it has been during the last decade. Very often the tackle used was of roughest and coarsest description; in some cases a length of twisted wire, armed with a big eel hook, did duty as bottom tackle, while as for the rod, I have seen weapons of fearful and wonderful construction, with butts like a 'weaver's beam,' and the running line itself has been watercord of the very thickest kind. Yet in those days of 'auld lang syne,' and with such tackle, huge barbel, and tremendous bags of them, have been hauled ashore; but nowadays a change has come over things. Skilled barbel fishers try to out-vie each other in the lightness of their rods, the thinness of their lines, and the fineness of their tackle; and even the barbel themselves have entered into the spirit of the thing, and will utterly refuse, in a general way, at any rate, all bait, unless it is offered to them on fine tackle, and in an artistic manner. Some odd times there is an exception to this rule, I am quite aware. Conditions of weather and water may be extra favourable, and some youngster, fishing with a stout string, a gimp hook, and the roughest of all lobworms, may land the barbel of the year. It has been done, and probably will again. But putting it as things generally go nowadays, if some of the old dead and gone school of Trent fishermen could only re-visit the scenes of their former triumphs, and try again with their old-time tackle, the result would utterly amaze them.

One of the very best bags of barbel that I have authentic information about was captured by poor old Owen, a former Newark tackle maker. Many years have passed since he was laid to his last rest. I remember the old chap and his funny little shop, hung round with curious old fishing prints. These memories stir up feelings that only anglers can appreciate. He pointed out to me with no little pride a page in his fishing journal, and let me copy it. It was a short account of the very best day's barbel fishing he ever enjoyed on the Trent. I find on reference that nearly fifty years have passed and gone since that, for him, eventful day. His bag had in it 32 barbel, five of which weighed from 12 to 15lb each; about a dozen more ranged from 6 to 10lb each, and the remainder were between 3 and 6lb each, the whole lot going no less than 224lb, being an average of 7lb per fish - a most extraordinary bag, and yet got with tackle and the like of which is not seen nowadays: tackle of such strength and thickness that when a barbel, no matter how big, was hooked, it has to come ashore without much ceremony. I may have seen one or two lots of barbel that exceeded Owen's in number, but I certainly never did see a bag that contained anything like such large fish. We must not nowadays expect a bag of that quality and dimensions; in fact, I should question if any angler during the last fifteen years has, in a single day's barbel fishing on the Trent, made a bag of over twenty fish that exceeded 3lb per fish. I once saw a bag made by three Nottingham fishermen from the Stoke waters, that contained fifty barbel, and the whole lot only weighed 72lb. On the other hand, the late Tom Bentley and myself once took a dozen fish from the same waters one afternoon that ranged from 5lb to 3½lb per fish. In direct opposition to this the same anglers, fishing the swim opposite 'Ike's Hut,' below Newark, took a score one day nearly all of a size from 2 to 2½lb each - a very poor average. Only once did I see what was fairly entitled to be called a real big bag, and that was made at the 'Corporation

Fishery,' Winthorp. 'Old Kitty,' a Nottingham man, was the principal operator. Two Newark anglers and himself baited up the swim with nearly 1,000 large lob-worms a day for a whole week before the fish came on, and then for two days the biting was of the most glorious description. If my memory is to be trusted, the united bag of the three anglers exceeded 3cwt, and the average weight of the fish fairly went over 3lb; this was about eighteen years ago. Since that time I have seen small bags made, say from three to half a dozen fish, that would occasionally reach 6 or 7lb per fish; but generally this has been when the capture has been effected in the rushing, boiling waters under the apron of a weir hole; but fishing the ordinary swims in the river, the average lately has been very small indeed. I have an idea, somehow or other, that there are a good supply of large barbel in both the Trent and the Thames, and perhaps before long, as the preservation societies get more efficient in their work, the average weight of the barbel captured may go up, until it ultimately reaches the figure of thirty or forty years ago. I could give several more incidents that came under my own observation during a somewhat lengthy experience on this subject, but I think I have said enough to illustrate my point, and made it pretty clear to the tyro that he must not expect to equal the marvellous catches of bygone days.

The barbel is a distinguished member of the carp family, and is known scientifically as 'Cyprinus Barbatus,' or 'Barbus Vulgaris.' He derives his name from the peculiar beard or wattles that hang from his mouth. Walton says: 'With these beards or wattles he is able to take such a hold upon weeds or moss that the sharpest floods cannot move him from his position;' but with all due respect, I should say this is wrong. I have most carefully examined these barbules, or wattles, and cannot find that they are adapted for this purpose at all. They are neither strong hooks nor yet powerful suckers. They appear to be very delicate and sensitive feelers. The mouth of a barbel is situated very much underneath; that is, the top jaw is longer than the bottom one, thus giving him a sort of long, Roman nose, which seems to me to serve the same purpose as the snout of a pig. He is, generally speaking, a ground or bottom feeding fish, and as he often frequents the deepest and darkest parts of the river, these wattles tell him when he comes in contact with the small crustaceans, or minute shell fish that form a large part of his food, when, pig-like, he roots with his long nose among the sand and stones on the bottom. He is a nice-looking fish, when in good condition, possessed of a fair amount of personal beauty. The scales of his back and sides are a bright olive green, tinged with gold as they get nearer his white belly; while his large and powerful fins, especially his pectorals, anals, and ventrals are edged with a deep purplish red. All these combine to give him a very attractive appearance, and I must confess that I then look upon him with a good deal of admiration. One little drawback he has, and that is, if you look at him straight in the face, his long, downward-pointing nose, and his little dark eyes seem to strike you as having a very villainous look about them, or, at any rate, a very spiteful one; but this is only a minor point. Taking him all round I am very much in love with him.

This fish has an historic interest, inasmuch as it forms one of the quarterings on the coat of arms of Margaret of

Anjou, wife of Henry VI. This fact proves that the barbel has been a denizen of our English rivers for a lengthy period - probably for all time. Scholars agree that this fish is not mentioned in the writings of the ancient Greeks. The first notice of it appears in the works of the Latin author, Ausonius, who wrote about the fourth century. He uses these words: 'And thou, O Barbus, harassed by the narrow passes of the winding Saravus, after thou has descended a river of greater fame, more fully dost exercise spacious swimmings.' The barbel must have been highly esteemed during the reign of Queen Elizabeth, for we find that a statute law was passed in those days to the effect that anyone taking barbel of less than twelve inches in length, should pay 'twenty shillings,' and 'give up the fish so wrongfully taken, and the net or engine so unlawfully used.' That act has never been repealed, and, therefore, the angler of the present day is still liable to the same pains and penalties. But as a barbel of twelve inches does not weigh three-quarters of a pound, the restriction perhaps would never be put in force, as it is a well-known fact that very small barbel are seldom captured with a rod and line; indeed, I cannot remember ever taking one myself, or seen one taken of a less weight than just named.

Barbel abound in the warmer latitudes of Europe, being particularly plentiful in the rivers Danube and Rhine. In England they are by no means widely distributed, being found in very few rivers indeed, the Thames and the Trent begin the principal. I have heard it said that they do not occur in Scotland at all. In the Danube we hear of barbel reaching the extraordinary weight of 40 and 50lb, but in England we have nothing like that. I should say from 15 to

18lb would be the very outside weight. I remember Joe Corah once getting one in the grey dusk of a September morning that tipped the beam at 13lb, and another that poor old Frank Sims took with a lampern bait on a night-line, during the latter part of a warm October, that went within a trifle of 17lb. This latter was by far the largest that ever gladdened my own eyes, even if his death was a little ignominious. I once was present when the salmon net was drawn ashore, at a place known locally as 'the bottom of the rundals,' about three or four miles below Newark. The contents of that net was an eye-opener to me. There were three or four barbel that went 9 or 10lb apiece, a good 6lb chub, a bream of grand proportions, and a couple of roach that weighed 3lb each, and goodness only knows how many escaped through the meshes of the net, which were six inches from knot to knot, so nothing, unless it was very large indeed, could stop within it. I should have liked that sample of fish to put in a glass case, but the orders were all fish except salmon must be at once returned to the river. I don't mind owning to the fact that I watched those fish plunge into the depths with a deep sigh of regret. It was that experience that led me to the conclusion that large barbel were more plentiful in the Trent than we gave it - up to then - credit for holding. But these big fellows do not fall to the lot of the angler any day - not once in a lifetime, perhaps. If he gets a specimen of 9lb he must be satisfied as fishing goes nowadays.

The barbel is mostly found in the deepest parts of the river; he does not like either extreme heat or extreme cold. The month of June is an exception to this rule, however, for during that month, after the operation of spawning, they congregate in very considerable numbers on the shallows for the purpose of scouring themselves. I have seen shallows literally alive with them. There was one famous place, close to a railway bridge across the Trent, that was an especial favourite with the barbel. Anyone going across this bridge in the dusk of a june evening would be considerably startled by hearing a sudden and tremendous splash, as though a cart-load of bricks had been suddenly tipped into the river. This was a huge shoal of barbel in less than two feet of water, perhaps startled by a shadow thrown across the river, or perhaps leaping of their own sweet will. Anyhow, it would be difficult to believe that this noise could be made by scouring fish, unless we had ocular proof of the fact, and there would be no difficulty in this, as the splash would very soon be repeated. Barbel spawn about the latter part of May, and do not retire into their regular quarters - the deep holes - before July, and should most certainly not be taken before then. I am aware that numbers of barbel are taken during June and the beginning of July by anglers fishing the shallow slacks with the cad-bait; but, generally speaking, the fish are then dirty, slimy, and disagreeable. It delights in such places as under and about the woodwork of an old bridge, provided the water is tolerably deep; and he is also found in the rushing, boiling waters of a weir hole, and in deep and rapid streams, for his powerful fins enable him to stem the strongest current. A nice, moderately-flowing stream, with a good gravel bottom, is also a favourite haunt. Another good place is a deep hole or eddy, close to an abrupt bend in the river. At many of these bends the water rushes hard towards the bank, forming a shelf, and then flows outward again towards the centre of the river, leaving a nice deep curl or eddy on the inside of this stream. These are capital places to find barbel, as the nature of the stream is such that food is swept into the eddy; but as I proceed with the various methods of fishing for barbel I may again refer to this question. As anglers like to cook and eat their quarry, I should like to say a few words on the subject; but I am sadly afraid that as far as barbel are concerned many good words cannot be written. They are coarse, bony, watery, and flavourless, and in my opinion one of the worst of our fresh-water fish. Fishermen's wives who live on the banks of the river are adepts at serving up fish in an attractive manner; but they generally confess to being beaten by this one. On the other hand, I have known some who were fond of them. The French hold them in esteem, storing them up in water-cages ready for use. Personally I have had them cooked, and find the best plan, if the fish is a small one, say from two to three pounds, is to cut off its head and fins, carefully remove its insides, clean and scale thoroughly, rub a little salt on it, and set it on one side for four or five hours; after this interval take a sharp knife, and split it down the back, removing the backbone (a good deal like filleting a sole), cut each half in two, and fry with a lump of good lard in a frying pan over a brisk fire; turn each piece over till both sides are nicely crisp and brown, and if well cooked the dish will be passable. If the barbel is a large one, say five or six pounds, it must be carefully cleaned, as recommended before, and salt rubbed in its inside. After the usual interval of four or five hours a good veal stuffing can be put in the inside, and all round it, and then baked in the oven. My opinion of this dish, however, is that the stuffing is the best part of him, especially if a bit of good bacon is cooked on the top of it. Some working men anglers will persist in cooking and eating the fish they catch, so I give what I consider to be the only plan of making this one anything like eatable; but one thing must be borne in mind, barbel must be cleaned as soon as possible after capture - an interval, say, of twenty-four hours between capture and cleaning will render him utterly unfit for the table. I have heard it said that the roe is poisonous.

And now, as a wind up to this chapter, I should like to make a personal explanation. I am not writing these pages for the benefit of very clever anglers, it is the novice and the working men anglers who are not above taking a few hints from a brother working man that I want to specially benefit if I can. I have some ground to traverse, and a lot of details to carefully note, for I take it that for a book to be practical and useful all minor details must be noted, and nothing, however small, that bears upon the question must be left out. Barbel fishing in all it branches contains a whole host of these little things, that collectively go towards making the expert angler. I must just give one word of warning, however, and that is, you must not expect to catch barbel, or I mean a fair good bag of them, every time you go barbel fishing. Even the expert 'barbeler' has to put up with full half a dozen disappointments to every one success. It is an uncertain job, and even when a pitch has been well baited the barbel may refuse to come on after all, although other fish in the swim will partly repay the angler for his trouble. Years ago they were nearly always 'on' during the months of August and September, and sometimes all through October, but of late years they are more often off than on; but when they do come on the fisherman is fully rewarded for any amount of past disappointment. The sport is glorious, and he will go again and again, buoyed up with hope that the experience may be repeated.

CHAPTER II

THE ROD, REEL AND LINE

The Barbel Rod - The Landing Net - The Reel - The Line

Barbel fishermen appear to me to be divided into certain classes, each class having a separate and distinct method of its own. Of course, there are some anglers, I am well aware, that are not tied to any one particular plan, but will adapt themselves to any circumstances, and try all possible ways to effcct a capture; but, speaking generally, as far as my own observation goes, I find that one man will swear by a certain method, and another by something else, and yet a third by something different still. These fishermen are divided into three classes: one will use extremely light tackle and a quill float, and swim the streams with a worm for bait; another class will use heavier tackle and the ledger, and for bait, scratchings, tallow cake, or greaves, whichever name that lure is known by in his own particular district, while the third class adopt a sort of compromise between the other two, and use a set of tackle that is called in some places long-corking, or tight-corking, and in others stret-pegging tackle. These three are the plans generally followed by barbel fishermen, and I will try to explain, as well as I can, in the following chapters the modus operandi of them all.

The first thing a barbel fisherman should select is his rod, and as this is by far the most important item in his outfit, it behoves him to use a considerable amount of judgement in the selection thereof. He must bear in mind the fact already hinted at in the first chapter, that he has a very powerful fish to cope with, that his hunting grounds, or waters, rather, are very often deep and strong streams, that obstructions in the shape of large stones or sunken timber very often mar his progress. Sometimes he may find it necessary to fish in the boiling waters of a weir hole, or among the piles and timbers of an old wooden bridge; and then, again, he will often find it expedient to swim his bait, strike, and play his quarry in a strong current at least twenty, thirty, or even forty yards away from where he stands. As it is absolutely necessary to fish on the bottom, his hook and bait may get fixed and immovable in an old snag, and considerable force has to be applied to break loose. All these things have to be taken into consideration when a rod is selected. I don't recommend a heavy, clumsy weapon, nor do I favour a very light one. It should be, in my opinion, about midway between the two. Some anglers are wonderfully fond of fishing with the very lightest rod they can procure, and the result is that when they come to use it ledgering in a weir hole it gets twisted up into all sorts of shapes, and cannot stop a barbel when in full sail for its hover, or even check his speed a little. This is all very well for the rod maker, the more weapons the angler wears out the better it is for trade; but for my own part I may as well confess that when I get a rod that suits me I want it to last several seasons, and I also like to feel perfectly safe, and to know that my rod is not likely to play me false in a critical moment. I once saw and handled one of the old time barbel rods; it was built by poor old Corby, an amateur rod maker who lived a good many years ago in the old Northgate Almshouses, at Newark. It was a barbel rod, if you like, and must have weighed a long way on to three pounds. I confess I never before or since saw its like; it must have been at least twenty years old when I saw it, and the old chap told me it had killed some scores and scores of big barbel. It was wonderfully thick in the butt, and not short of timber in the top either, for the matter of that; but it must be remembered that the rod was designed when lines were made of stout water-cord, tackle of twisted copper wire, and barbel hauled ashore without much ceremony. Later on I saw that rod in the hands of a noted pike fisher; he was dead-gorging with it among the reeds and weeds of a backwater, and the user assured me that when in conflict with a heavy jack it was the most punishing rod he ever had in his life. There was something about that rod that struck me very favourably. I could see in my mind's eye how it would bend to the strong pull of a ten-pounder, and it set me thinking. Now I am not going to recommend a weapon of this calibre, nor yet one of its very great weight; but I am going to take it as a model, and reduce the material throughout, and bring it to the requirements of the present school of barbel fishermen, and the result will be, in my opinion, a barbel rod par excellence. I have seen a good many barbel rods in my time in the hands of some of the most experienced working men anglers on the Trent, and they all seem to be actuated by one motive: that is, the rod must be no heavier than is absolutely necessary; it much be nice and stiff, with a strike that is direct from the point, and it also must be well set up in its joints.

A fair good grip of timber in the hand seems also to be another favourite attribute. I at once pronounce in favour of a Nottingham pattern for this work; none others, in my opinion, are anything like so good. The length need not be much over twelve feet, if any, and the weight should not be less than eighteen ounces, nor need it be more than twenty-one. I am strongly in favour of this rod being in no more than three lengths. The butt should be made from a length of good old seasoned red deal, straight in the grain, tough in texture, and free from curls and knots. When I say red deal, I don't mean any sort of wood you could pick up in a joiner's shop, but genuine red deal. I have spent half a day in a large timber merchant's yard, and turned over some scores of planks, before I could find half a dozen that suited me. The middle joint should be of the same material and lancewood spliced together in a long fish splice. Poor old Corby's splice was exactly in the centre of the joint, and was no less than thirty inches long, or more than half the entire length of the joint itself. The ferrule on the butt should measure about three-quarters of an inch in diameter, and the one on the centre joint about three-eighths of an inch, the reel fittings, or rather the wood close to the fittings, should be about three and a half inches in circumference, and the bottom ring of these fittings should not be less than eight inches from the end of the butt. The top joint should be made of good, tough lancewood. I don't like greenheart in a barbel rod, as that wood seems to me to have such an unpleasant knack of snapping short off, sometimes without any apparent reason. Personally, I like my lancewood top spliced and glued up in one or two places, and this splice should be a fair good length and whipped well. The top should be dressed down nice and fine towards the tip, so as to get the strike as direct and as prompt as possible. The rings on the whole rod should be fairly large, 'Bell's Life,' or safety guard pattern on the butt and middle joint, and steel snake rings on the top. The ordinary standup rings are not much good for the lower joints, as when casting out the float and bait, the line is liable to hitch or catch round them. My own favourite barbel rod is 12ft 6in long, but instead of having the glued up middle of hard wood, it has a length of very good and stiff East India cane, which is, in my opinion, an improvement, being a little lighter and a little stiffer. This rod has an extra top a foot shorter than the other, for heavy ledgering in rough water and weir holes. It weighs altogether, with both tops, 21oz, and as a good deal of this weight is in the lower end, it does not smack of top-heaviness at all, and can be used in perfect comfort on any barbel swim. A barbel rod must not wobble in the middle; I would much rather see the fault the other way, and have it extra stiff just there. It is astonishing the spring and resistance there is in a rod such as that just described, and in the play of the finely-dressed top. When in conflict with a big fish the rod should form a beautiful and perfect arch from about the centre of the middle joint round to the top ring, the lower half of it feeling stiff and rigid in the hand. If the weapon comes up to these requirements, and the angler displays anything like ordinary care in the playing, coupled with sound tackle, it will have to be an extra big fish that breaks away owing to a fault in the rod. This class of rod has the merit of being not very expensive, a good one will cost something like eight to twelve shillings, according to quality and finish;

and as it is to working men anglers that I am writing, this item of expense may be interesting. I have been rather particular in my remarks as to a rod, because I am very anxious that the would-be barbel fisherman should have some idea of his requirements when selecting this item for his outfit. I am in favour of using a barbel rod for the purpose of barbel fishing and nothing else; but if the angler cannot afford more than one rod, why, it has to be 'Hobson's choice' with him; but still, as I want to point out, a good barbel rod is rather too heavy for dace, roach, and chub fishing, and this is why I recommend a separate rod for the style of fishing now under notice.

Another very important item in a barbeller's outfit is a good landing net; in fact, in my opinion, no one should be without one, and as they can be procured at nearly any price the expense need not be too serious. I may as well say, however, that the plainer and stronger this article is the better. I recommend a fairly good one, for choice the handle should be of stout East India mottled cane, about $4^1/_2$ft long, bored out to hold either of the tops that are not just then in use. This is an advantage, as the spare top will be safer inside the handle than if it lay on the bank exposed to any careless foot that might by chance tread on it - I speak feelingly just now, as I have had more than one good rod top utterly ruined by being trodden upon as it lay on the gravel or grass by the riverside. There is a difference of opinion among anglers as to the best ring for the landing net; some swear by a wooden one, as they say, if by accident it is dropped into the river it will swim, and could be easily recovered, whereas an iron one would sink, and probably be lost for ever. There is something in this. Others will swear by a steel collapsing one, but in my humble opinion, for the sport now under review, nothing will beat a stout iron one. It should, however, be made with joints so as to fold up and pack away snug in the basket or bag when not in use; one about 16in in diameter is the most useful size, and the screw that fits into the socket at the end of the handle should be carefully examined from time to time to see that it fits close, and screws up tightly and well, as it is very annoying to have the net twist right round just when you are about to land a good fish. The net itself should be of good, stout material, and either tanned or waterproofed; the former is the cheapest, and, in my opinion, the best. This net should be at least 24in deep, and fairly roomy, as Mr. Barbel has an unpleasant knack of jumping out again if the net is too shallow and plate-like. A good landing net complete is rather an expensive item; one something like what I have just described would run to eight or nine shillings. A capital net can, however, be made by nearly any handy angler, a good broom stick, stained and varnished, or else painted green, about five feet of quarter-inch or five-sixteenths of an inch iron rod, bent in proper shape and bound tightly to the shaft, and the ordinary strong twine net being the whole of the articles required, and would form a very good makeshift, especially if the fisherman lived on the banks of a barbel river. I most certainly recommend the other one described, for the reasons already given, even if the expense is a little more.

Another absolute necessity in a barbel fisherman's kit is a good running reel, and I may as well say at once that a wooden Nottingham reel is far away the best. Three and a half or four inches in diameter is the most useful size, and it should be a good stout cross-back, and above all it must be very free and easy running. The barbel should revolve on the spindle without catch, jerk, or hindrance, nor should it wobble in the slightest. It does not matter for barbel fishing whether this reel is a centre pin or a plain spindle and nut reel, so long as it revolves with the utmost freedom. It can be fitted up with a moveable check action if the fisherman likes; this action may be of value sometimes, especially when ledgering, but personally I don't care for a check to my bottom fishing reels, preferring to check with my fingers. The spindle of this reel should be kept clean and well oiled, so as always to be in good working order. The same remark will also apply to the whole reel itself. It must be kept as clean and well polished as possible, and above all, after using, especially when wet, it must be dried carefully, and kept in a place free from damp, or the wood will warp and stick. A good, useful barbel reel can be bought very cheaply nowadays; in fact, for as low as half-a-crown, but as this is an item that with care will last for years, it will be as well to have a fairly good one for a start.

With regard to a line for barbel fishing, there seems to be a difference of opinion amongst anglers. Some say a twisted silk is the best, while others favour a plaited silk. I am in favour of the latter, as I fancy it has a little more strength to a little less bulk, and is not so liable to kink, or hold water as that which is twisted. This line need not be too thick and stout; in fact, the finer it is the better, consistent with strength. It is rather difficult to give an idea on paper as to the proper size of these lines, but they are about as thick as very coarse sewing thread. The size of line I like is Messrs. Allcock's No. 6 or No. 5, of plaited, undressed silk. The No. 6 is about as fine as is safe to use; for float fishing it is a very good line, and with care will kill almost anything in reason, besides being a capital one for throwing out a bait and swimming down the stream. A yard of this line will lift five pounds dead weight without breaking, so when we take into account the spring of the rod this would be much increased when wet and in use. As a general barbel line, perhaps, the No. 5 will be found the best. At any rate, for ledgering it would be. This line will lift 8lb dead weight. For float fishing with a small swan quill float it is rather too coarse; but for stret-pegging with a heavy cork float it is all right, and very safe line, especially if heavy barbel are expected in the swim operated on. The angler should have not less than 60, nor need he have more than 100 yards wound on his reel, and with this quantity he will be ready for any emergency. The barbel line should be slightly dressed, so as to float on the surface of the water. There are two or three things that will answer this purpose - a slight dressing of King's ceroleum is one good thing, vaseline is another, and a well-known Nottingham angler recommends most strongly a bit of parrafine wax. This can be got for a trifle at any chemist's, and when rubbed down the line causes it to float. This is a great advantage when swimming a stream, which I shall fully explain in another chapter.

CHAPTER III

ON BARBEL FLOATS

The swan quill - The pelican quill - How to make a float - Varnish - Cork floats - The Slider float - Composite floats.

In this chapter I propose to describe the floats that are used in barbel fishing, including all that can possibly be required under any circumstances, and any description and conditions of water, stream, and locality. There is more in this question of floats than is apparent to the novice at first sight. He might think that any sort of a float would do, so long as it was one, and that the one float would do for any sort of barbel fishing; but I must at once dispel this idea, and say that it is to a most careful selection of his floats - a proper one for certain conditions of water - that his success as a barbel fisherman in a great measure depends. I am anxious to give this novice a few hints and a little information that will enable him to make some of his floats, and also be useful to him when buying the rest. I don't intend at this stage to go into a discussion as to the superiority of the float tackle over the ledger, or whether, on the other hand, the ledger is far away better than the float. Some men favour the one and utterly condemn the other. I am not one of these. I have found both methods work well. The angler should, as it were, take stock of his surroundings, carefully note the character of the stream, be guided by any chance information he can pick up on the banks, even from the most unlikely sources, keep his eyes well open, and after a little preliminary trial he will soon find out whether the ledger is likely to be the correct card, or if the float tackle is most likely to succeed. I will say no more just now on the vexed question of float versus ledger, but will most carefully note it when I come to describe each plan, and perhaps my few hints may help the fisherman to decide for himself which is likely to be the most profitable in the swim he happens just then to find himself on.

In introducing the subject of floats, I may say that those highly-coloured - green, blue, and red - thick-bellied ones, with a wooden shank through them (somewhat in the shape of a schoolboy's peg-top), which the novice sometimes sees displayed so very temptingly in some fishing-tackle shop windows, I will at once dismiss from my list, and warn the novice that no matter how useful he might have found them in his youthful days when trying for perch in some pond, they are no good for barbel fishing. He must have something that offers less resistance to the stream when winding his line home again for a fresh cast. Large quills and thin cork ones are the best, and in order to simplify matters as I go along I will number the floats as I describe them, so as to make it easier for future reference. My readers must bear in mind that in the remaining chapters on barbel fishing, when I have occasion to refer to a certain float, I shall do so by simply quoting the number as given in this chapter.

No. 1. Is a fair-sized swan quill, about eight inches in length, and capable of carrying eight fair-sized split shots.

This float should be made from one of the largest, soundest, and roundest quills from the wings of a swan. A cap should be fixed at one end, and a small brass ring at the other. This float is used in swims where the water is not above six feet in depth, and the stream fairly steady; or when the river has run down to its lowest summer level, is very clear and stagnant, and not above half the current of ordinary times. More especially is it useful during the early part of the season, when the barbel are in shallow places or odd, quiet corners, and a couple of cad baits the best bait that can be offered to them.

No. 2. Is a large pelican quill, nine or ten inches long, and buoyant enough to allow a dozen large shot to be put on the tackle. This is my favourite float for fishing swims moderate as to flow. Such quill floats are rather expensive; I have given as much as ninepence and a shilling for one in the rough, but if you get hold of a good one it is cheap at nearly any price, as they are first-class floats for fishing any ordinary barbel swim. As these floats are easy to make, I will give here a few hints as to their manufacture, and hope it won't be considered in the nature of a digression. Anyhow, I think it will be useful; at any rate, I should have welcomed the information at one time. Procure some good swan and pelican wing feathers, and choose those that are straight, clean, thick in the barrel, and round; carefully examine them to see that there are no holes or cracks, particularly in the barrel end. If the inspection is satisfactory, take a very sharp pocket-knife and cut half of the feather end clean off (each end of the float, barrel end and feather end, should be about as long as one another); then take hold of the top or round end of the quill and scrape downwards with your knife towards the end where the ring wants to be, taking care that all the feather is scraped off, and no cuts or jags appear on it. Then turn it end for end, and repeat the operation on the top part, but don't scrape too deep - just the surface is capable of being cut very thin. From the front or pith part you remove about three-quarters of an inch, leaving the back intact, but as thin as you can pare it. This will bend over, leaving a sort of eye at the extreme end; a small brass ring can be inserted in this eye, and a bit of waxed silk binds all down neat and secure. The amateur float-maker can also bind a narrow ring of silk in two or three places round it if he likes. I don't know that it is of any advantage, but it gives the float a more finished appearance. Every fisherman ought to possess a bottle of good spirit varnish, it comes in handy for a variety of purposes. A good bottle of varnish can be made very cheaply thus: - Three ounces of the best wood naptha in a doctor's medicine bottle; two ounces of the best yellow gum shellac; and one ounce of gum benzine. These last two items should be finely pounded up, and put in the bottle among the naphtha, and shaken frequently. In three or four days the gums will have dissolved; strain through a bit of muslin so as to remove the sediment from the benzine, and pour back into the bottle. This is a thick, sticky liquid, capital for painting over whippings and the like. It is, however, rather too thick for painting over the body of the float, so I recommend half of this varnish to be put in another bottle and another ounce of the naphtha mixed with it. The angler will then have two bottles - one thick, the other thin. The camel-hair brushes that he applies the varnish with, can be fastened in the cork of the bottles, so as to be always ready for use. A thin coat can be applied to the whole float, and if he gives it three coats at intervals of a day between each one it will be all the better, taking care to do as I have just hinted. Put the thick varnish on the whippings, and the thin on the float itself. The whole cost of these two bottles will not exceed a shilling; the ingredients can be bought at any chemist's. I should have said just now that in varnishing his float about an inch at the tip end should not be so done, as I like this coloured a brilliant red. The best thing for the purpose is a pinch of powdered vermillion mixed in three or four drops of the before-mentioned varnish, and applied with another small brush. After the red tip is quite dry, and it should not be longer than two or three hours, another brushing over it with the thin varnish finishes the business. Cork floats are much more difficult to make; in fact, I don't recommend the novice to try his hand on them, as they can be bought even cheaper than good quills; but he wants to know the exact sort, so I will describe.

No. 3. Which is a cork float of the pattern usually found in the tackle cases of Nottingham fishermen. This float is generally about eight inches or so long over all, the cork part forming about half of its entire length only. The cork should be thickest in the middle, from five-eighths to three-quarters of an inch in diameter will be ample, and tapered towards each end. The great peculiarity of these floats, and one that enables the tyro to easily recognise them, is the shape of the quill that runs through the centre. It is not straight, like a porcupine quill, but bent in a slight curve, and for this purpose turkey quills are used in the manufacture of the best. The wing feathers of the turkey are bent rather more than either swan or pelican feathers. For stream fishing a cork float of this shape seems to possess a decided advantage over one that is perfectly straight. The quill that projects above the cork should be about one and a half inches long, tipped with red, and about two and a half inches of quill, with a brass ring at the extreme end, should project below the cork at the bottom end. This is an extremely useful float for the barbel fisher, and will be found very serviceable in a variety of circumstances, especially if a fairly strong stream is running, and an extra amount of lead has to be put on the tackle for the purpose of well holding the bottom with the bait.

No. 4. Is a similar float to the foregoing; exactly in the same shape, but, say, a couple of sizes larger, and capable of carrying a fair amount of split shot, and also a corking lead. This latter article, I may say in passing, is a lead weight about an inch long and a quarter of an inch or so in diameter, slightly tapered towards each end, with a small hole running lengthways through it. Its use will be explained in its proper place. This No. 4 float is used for long-corking and tight-corking, or, as it is known on the Trent, 'stret-pegging,' and it will also come in handy for fishing in the rough water below a weir, or in the deep holes formed in flood times by the scour and rush of the water below the falls.

No. 5. Is the slider, or, as it is known on the Trent, 'the running float.' As its name indicates, this float is so constructed that it runs, or slides, up and down the line. It sometimes happens that the swim operated on is from fourteen to twenty feet deep; indeed, I am acquainted with one swim on the Trent that is not less than thirty feet deep during its lowest summer level. It must be patent to the veriest novice that to fish a swim thirty feet deep with a fixed float and a twelve-foot rod would be an utter impossibility. If by some chance the bait and float did manage to get into their proper positions, and a barbel was hooked, how could it be landed? The fixed float would be jammed up tight against the top ring of the rod, and the fish still a dozen feet below the surface, and no earthly chance of getting it any nearer unless the rod was laid on the bank and the line pulled in hand over hand, which operation would not be very successful, I should say, as far as barbel were concerned. I remember once, a good few years ago now, a question being asked by a correspondent in the columns of a sporting paper. It was in the days when this style of fishing was not generally understood, even by experienced men, to say nothing of the great bulk of anglers. If I recollect aright, the question was something like this: 'Can a barbel swim, say twenty feet deep, be fished with an ordinary twelve-foot rod and float tackle, and if so how is it to be done?' I remember the reply of the gentleman whose duty it was to answer these questions. He said: 'As far as I can see, it would be an impossibility, unless the angler had a big tree and a long ladder directly at his back, so that on hooking a barbel he could mount the tree the requisite height, while a companion below landed the fish.' That reply at the time struck me as being remarkably ingenious, and showed a fertility of thought that was positively refreshing. It is said that the celebrated 'Nottingham George,' an angler who has been dead some years, was the inventor of the 'slider' float. He was probably the most successful barbel fisherman that ever lived. This old angler left his native Trent many years ago and settled at Windsor, on the Thames. Many anglers now living can remember the quaint old man and his sayings. He graduated on the Trent, as I have just observed, and was brought up in the midst of a splendid school of piscators who, as yet knowing little or nothing of the principles of fine Thames ledger-fishing, pinned their faith almost entirely to the float. I cannot do better than give the story of the invention of this float in the words of a man who interviewed 'Old George,' and gave the results of that interview in an obscure journal several years ago, under the title of 'Recollections of Nottingham George.' 'There was one great deep full of grand barbel, and, as George said, it was literally impossible to fish it, at any rate for very far beyond the brow of the hole, consequently the big fish lying in the very depths of the hole escaped all the pains and penalties incident to a love of bright, well-scoured lobworms; and whether it was crafty old George, or indeed anyone else, who essayed the capabilities of this locality, they invariably escaped scot free. If my memory serves me correctly, this deep was situated in the Collingham waters, below Newark; and one night George woke his wife up in a tremendous hurry, saying, "Eh! missus, missus! I've had a wonderful dream. I've found out how to fish the big hole at Collingham!" "Thou hast, lad? Well, prithee get up and go and fish it," was his wife's suggestion, doubtless vexed at being woke up from deep sleep. "And," said George, "I jumped up, full of my new idea, which came to me in a dream, and I roughly rigged up a big float, such as I used to work for stret-pegging, with two rings top and bottom, and with a bit of a stop on my silk line wound upon the barrel of my reel, and stood by daybreak on the banks of the big pool. That morning was to be either a great triumph for me or a dismal failure. I cannot tell you what I thought when I saw the float slipping up the line foot after foot, as the sharp stream swept it over the brow of the hole, and presently stand pretty nigh motionless in the very centre of the deep eddy. I had only got to slip my bit of silk stop down to a foot above where the running line was wet, and then I knew I'd got the right depth, and presently I began to scatter the worms in; and, my sakes! by night-time there was such a sight of great fish on the Trent bank as I don't believe was ever seed before, and all the chaps were talking and babbling about me, and a wondering how I'd done it." This appears to me to be the history of the invention of the Nottingham 'slider' float; at any rate it is generally accepted as a fact by many of the Trent men. To make this float I recommend a very large one of the sort already described as No. 2; but instead of the cap fitting tightly at the top end, an ordinary fair-sized upright rod ring should be substituted. This ring must be whipped on firmly with well-waxed silk about an inch from the red tip. Directly opposite this ring, at the other end of the float, another very small ring should be whipped on. This small ring should only be just large enough to easily thread the barbel line through - a bit of fine brass wire is used for the purpose. Wind a length of this wire two or three turns round a stout needle and draw off; cut each end to about half an inch in length, and bend at right angles, exactly like an ordinary upright ring. These ends are to bind the ring to the float. If these rings are properly put on they should stand exactly opposite each other, the larger one about an inch from the top of the float, and the tiny one a similar distance from the bottom end. Now take your barbel line and thread the end through the large ring, then through the small one, and see if the float will easily drop down. Hold the line fairly tight with hands about a yard apart, and move first one hand at top, then the other, and if the float slips easily from one hand to the other it is correctly made. A very little bit of a loop on the line will stop the float anywhere, and this loop should be no larger than is actually required, so that it will run without hindrance through the rings on the rod, and yet stop the float on the line exactly at the depth you put it. The loop must be just large enough, so as to prevent it from being drawn through the little ring on the float, and no more. If you are fishing a hole, say, twenty feet deep, you first of all thread the line through the two float rings, as already indicated; then tie your shotted and weighted tackle to the line, carefully measure the exact depth, and make the loop in your line as high up as required. When making your cast the float, of course, has dropped down to the loop of the tackle at its juncture with the silk line. As soon as the cast is made the weighted tackle sinks towards the bottom, but the float keeps on the surface, the rings allowing the line to travel through until the float reaches the stop-loop already indicated, and cannot go further. When playing a fish, as you wind him nearer the surface, the float, of course, drops down again towards the gut tackle, and is always out of the way, and there is no question of it jamming up against the rod top. I think this makes it pretty clear to the novice as to the use and utility of the 'slider' float. I have long considered this float as being one of the most useful a fisherman can have. A capital slider can also be made out of the No. 4 stret-pegging float already described; indeed, I am not certain that this float would not be the most useful of the two as a general slider. In certain swims it would, at any rate, for instance, if a long distance had to be cast, where it would be necessary to throw the bait direct from the reel, the same as casting out a spinning bait for pike, or where the hole was very deep, and a heavy curl in the water. The directions already given for making the one will answer admirably for the other, except in the case of the ring near the top end, an ordinary upright rod ring will not do for a cork float. This ring should have a long neck, so that the eye of the ring stands a full half-inch above the quill on which it is bound; you see the cork is thick in the middle, and if the ring did not project pretty prominently when the line is tight and wet it would stick to the centre of the cork and hinder its free running; otherwise its make and use are exactly as already fully described. I strongly recommend the would-be barbel fishermen to have both the No. 2 and the No. 4 floats fitted up as 'sliders.' These half-dozen floats are about all that the barbel fishermen require. I have seen and used floats of curious construction, some of them none the less useful for all that. One of the very best I ever saw was made from the large quill of an albatross - an extraordinary buoyant float that would carry an amazing amount of lead. This was the favourite float of the late Tom Rudd, who was for many years the landlord of the 'Reindeer Inn,' and one of the best barbel fishers I ever came across. A very good one that I used at times for years was made out of three very large swan quills, carefully joined together and whipped every half-inch from end to end with well-waxed silk. This one I fitted up as a slider, and found it a capital float for fishing very deep waters. The way I joined those three quills together was this: After cutting the proper length and scraping, I boiled them for a few minutes, to render them pliable; while hot they were put together with the hollow sides facing each other, and a bit of fine twine wound round them to bring all close together. Remove this twine when cold, and whip as just directed, finally varnishing and painting all over thoroughly. I have seen barbel floats made from reed with the ends plugged up, but I did not think much of them. Composite floats that are made one part quill, one part reed, and still another part wood, that have to be joined together in sections, are treacherous, owing to their liability to get water-logged at the various joints. I once saw a float made of strips of quill, put round an elongated indiarubber bag filled with gas; but I did not favour that idea, as a very little accident might damage the bag and spoil it for ever. Taking them all round I most decidedly favour the whole quill or the Nottingham cork, when used as floats for barbel fishing.

CHAPTER IV

BARBEL TACKLE AND HOW TO MAKE IT

Silkworm gut - Stains - Knots - Tying silk and hooks - White wax - Hook tying - Float and tackle case - Bags and baskets.

Tackle for barbel fishing should be made from the very best silkworm gut it is possible to buy. Some of my correspondents at various times have been labouring under the idea that this gut is cat-gut; but for the information of all such I may say that it is procured from the silkworm. Immense quantities of these worms are bred and fed at Murcia, in Spain. At a certain stage of the caterpillar's growth they are thrown into some boiling liquid; the inside of the worm is then drawn out, which, after drying and other processes, becomes the angler's gut of commerce. I am very fond of fine tackle myself, and like to fish very fine; but in the case of the barbel it will be found a mistake to use it too extra fine, for various reasons. I have hinted in the first chapter that this fish is a rare fighter, and very powerful, that his home is in rapid currents, deep holes, alongside the woodwork of old bridges, against stone walls, the rough water of a weir, etc.; and as the stream sweeps all sorts of small things into the eddies formed by those places, perhaps the barbel do not notice so very minutely such a thing as a bit of gut rolling along the bottom; anyhow, my opinion is that the gut is not so particular as if you were fishing for roach in very still and very clear water. At the same time we must give the barbel credit for being anything but a fool; and must use tackle no coarser in substance than is absolutely required for safety. It is not advisable to use drawn gut for barbel tackle, because this gut has one serious disadvantage when fished down a deep rapid stream with a fair sized hook and bait on it; sometimes, when winding the line home again after an extra long swim, this drawn gut twists up; and instead of the hook and bait hanging clear at the extreme end, they are a couple of feet up the tackle, and tightly twisted round the shots. I am of the opinion that this is caused by the gut during manufacture being drawn through small holes in a brass or steel plate; this is a process of the makers for thinning it; (and is the reason why this gut is known to the trade as drawn gut); this operation must of necessity stretch it, and by being wound rapidly against the stream when in use causes it to curl or twist up; this peculiarity is more to be observed when the tackle is heavily shotted, the bait a good sized one, and the swim heavy and deep. For stream fishing for any sort of fish, I always prefer undrawn gut; and for the barbel this preference is of a more decided character. The quality of gut known to dealers as 'First Padron' is far the best for the fish now under notice. Some anglers are wonderfully fond of making their own tackle; they say it seems to add to the enjoyment of the thing if the capture is successfully effected on tackle of their own manufacture; I will give a few hints as to how it should be done. A real good hank, consisting of a hundred strands of first quality Padron gut thirteen inches long can be bought for half-a-crown; cheap enough in all conscience. Before these strands of gut are tied together in lengths, I always consider it necessary to stain them. Some anglers say they are better without staining, and go into experiments to prove their position, such as putting two strands of gut, one natural, the other stained, into a glass globe or bowl of water and holding it above their heads to the light; they say the unstained one shows less in the water than the stained; but it appears to me that two or three other items should be taken into consideration before deciding this point. Supposing the angler could experiment at the bottom of the river, and look at those two lengths of gut with a background of blue sky against him, I fancy the one stained a light blue would show less in the water than the one that was white, whatever the latter might do if the bowl was held up in a room with only a background of white ceiling against it. Beside the sky there would in many places be a background of trees, bushes, and weeds; or it may be in the gloomy depths under a bridge. Stained gut at any rate would be likely to show less in the water than gut left a transparent white. Barbel appear to me from the position and formation of their snouts and mouths to be fish who grope and feel about the bottom of the river for their food, that is, speaking generally: so perhaps they do not take much notice of such a thing as a bit of gut floating in mid-water above them. Then again, I remember an instance, the results of which were a bit of a poser. A youth and I went down the Trent one day to try a hole for barbel; the water was wonderfully low and clear. We ledgered with scratchings for bait, at least my companion did, all through the day; I varied the programme somewhat, rung the changes from that bait to worms, tried floating; long-corking; then back to the ledger. I used gut tackle stained blue, then changed to orange coloured, and finally white, and as fine as I dare, considering the nature of the swim. My youthful friend had an idea of his own; he wanted 'summat to hode em,' as he himself expressed it. His ledger was a home-made lead plumb at least a couple of ounces in weight; his line was of the substance of a pike line while the tackle itself was simply eighteen inches of stout white gimp, mounted with a rusty No. 1 Carlisle hook. I should not have dreamed of using gimp above half that thickness for jack fishing: but mark the result: I got a fair bag of various fish, but only one barbel; a miserable three-pounder; the youth got four good fish, two six-pounders, a five, and a four. This result rather upset my theory on the subject of fine tackle in connection with barbel fishing, and seemed to favour the opinion of another old angling friend, who would have it that 'the fishermen were a lot more particular than the fish.' But on the other hand I can remember a case that was exactly the other way about; another old fisherman and myself were trying a swim from a boat, we were supposed to be dace fishing, the stream had a beautiful sandy bottom, was about twelve feet deep in front of the boat; but at the end of the swim, some twenty yards lower down stream; it suddenly shoaled off, to about six feet: there being a sort of ledge there that could not be reached from the bank; of course our tackle was made suitable for dace out of the very finest drawn gut; we used cad-baits as a lure; and found during the course of the day, that when the bait travelled to the end of the swim; and reached that ledge, we now and again got a sudden and sharp bite, followed by a heavy tug; and a lost hook; at last after a bit of careful play I managed to land one of those fish that had been playing such unkind pranks with our gut lines, and found it to be a barbel, a little over four pounds; and probably one of the smallest in the hole; we now thought it time to alter our tackle, and put on stouter; but after an hour's careful trial we failed to get another bite; we then went back to the extra fine tackle and small hooks; and the very first swim down resulted in another smashed tackle. This was to say the least of it rather peculiar; and for once in a way we had happened to drop across some barbel that could distinguish between stout tackle and fine. Here are two cases picked at random out of an experience extending to many years; which are exactly opposed to each other; and the moral of it appears to be; 'Be on the safe side, use tackle no coarser than is absolutely required.' There is one thing to be said in favour of fine tackle when barbelling, and that is, you can fish your swim so much easier; you can float down the stream with much more comfort, and last, but not least, in making your cast you can throw much further and cleaner, with less friction and jerk with a moderately fine line and tackle than you can with a very coarse one. I most decidedly hold to the opinion that good stout chub tackle is plenty strong enough to kill barbel. If your gut line will lift, say from three to four pounds from the ground without breaking, it is all right. The quality and brand of the gut already recommended will do this very comfortably. When you have made a purchase of this hank of gut, you will notice some red material like coarse thread wound tightly round one end, and at the other end it is fluffy, curly, and finer in texture. These two ends should be cut off and thrown away, being useless for barbel tackle, the thirteen or fourteen inches in the middle only being used. The first process of the amateur tackle maker is to stain this gut; but I was nearly forgetting a small item, but none the less important, for all that; the quality of gut now under notice is generally sold as 'picked gut,' that is, carefully sorted before being tied up in hanks, only perfect and sound lengths being selected. But in case any imperfect strands should by mistake be included, they must be promptly rejected. Gut that is flat and irregular in places, with spots of dull chalky white on its surface, should not be used by the careful man; it ought to present a bright and glossy appearance. It is not absolutely necessary that every length should be perfectly round, so long as it is regular and equal in size from end to end and perfectly sound. A most useful and cheap stain for gut, and one that is very easy in application, is a sixpenny bottle of Judson's dyes; this can be procured from the nearest chemist; the colour known as Oxford blue gives the gut as good a natural water colour as any I know, and is one I strongly recommend for staining barbel tackle. Another good dye is light brown, or perhaps orange. These give a tint closely resembling the sand and gravel on the bottom of the river. The first step is to prepare the stain, and for this purpose a pint of clean boiling water should be poured in a bowl; immediately the contents of the bottle must be added and stirred well about with a stick, set it on one side to cool, and when cold put the whole in a clean wine bottle and cork down. It is then ready for use, and will keep good for a twelvemonth or more. To stain the gut take a teacup full of the mixture out of the bottle and add to it two teacupfuls of clean, cold water. Put these in an old iron saucepan or a tin egg-boiler, and stir well so that the liquid is well mixed; then put the gut in carefully, so that every portion is covered by the stain; set the vessel on a slow fire till its contents boil; let it boil one minute, - no longer - then lift the gut out with an old spoon, or something similar, and instantly plunge it in another vessel of cold water. This sets the stain. Wash the gut well, and the operation is complete. The quantities of water and stain that I have given makes a capital tint, not too dark in colour; but if the operator thinks the quantities are not enough to well cover his gut, he must increase it, still keeping to the same proportions as just mentioned. It is the best to tie gut together when wet and thoroughly soaked, as it is too brittle to knot together when dry; in fact, a secure knot cannot be tied in dry gut - as soon as it is pulled up tight it breaks. I recommend the novice to sort out as many strands as he requires in two lots. Some of these strands may be thicker than others. These should be put in a bowl of water by themselves, and the thinner ones in another vessel. By this means the tackle can be tapered, the stouter at the top end and the finer towards the hook. Clean, cold water is the best to soak gut in; and if it stops in the water for half a day, or even more, it will take no hurt; in any case, a few minutes will not do, it must have time to thoroughly soften. I should say a couple of hours is the very least time to allow it to become pliable in. There are several methods of tying a good tackle knot. I will explain two only, which, in my opinion, are best for the purpose. The first is generally called the 'fisherman's knot,' which has the merit of being very simple and easy, is not very wasteful of material, does not show too prominently, and above all is pretty firm and secure, without much chance of slipping undone at a critical moment. To tie this knot the operator takes a strand of gut and ties a single knot at the end, or nearly so, but without pulling it tight, so that it forms a sort of eye. Now take another length and thread one end through the eye or loop already made in the first one, tie a similar loop or single knot round the first length with the end of the second, take hold of the short end of each knot separately and pull tight, finally catching hold of each long end and drawing both together firm and secure, and clipping off the spare short ends to about a quarter of an inch from the knot. This fastening has just one little drawback: sometimes one part of the knot will jam itself nearly under the other part, and draw in too tight, especially if one strand is very much finer than the other, and in time cuts itself out. Once or twice I have had this accident happen to my tackle; but, generally speaking, when the gut is fairly stout, and the two lengths of a thickness, the knot is a pretty safe one. The other one is known as the 'tacklemaker's knot,' and is perhaps the soundest that can be tied. It is, however, very wasteful, and does not look quite so neat as the other one. It is tied by placing the ends of two strands together, of course each end pointing in opposite directions. To successfully do it, it is necessary that the ends should overlap each other at least two inches, and both tied together by the simple loop or knot; but instead of only being put through once, it should be done so twice, and then drawn up tight and secure. The spare ends of this knot can be clipped close off. This is a splendid knot, in spite of its rather clumsy look, and is what I strongly recommend the novice to adopt in making his barbel tackle, as there is no question about its strength and soundness if properly tied. It will pay the amateur at first to practice with a bit of fine twine, until he gets into the twist of the thing, or he may waste several lengths of his more valuable gut. Float fishing and long-corking tackle for this fish should have five lengths of gut in it, and be at least four feet long, with a loop securely tied at either end, care being taken that the very stoutest lengths are at the end furthest from the hook. Some anglers whip the hook direct on the end of the tackle, and only have one loop at the opposite end; but I like the hook itself to be on a separate length, so that in case of an accident to the hook, or a change is required, the whole of the properly shotted tackle need not be removed. If there is a loop securely whipped at the end of the hook length of gut, it can be joined to or taken from the main gut line with the greatest ease and quickness. This plan is also a great saving of tackle, because the bottom length of gut is liable to get worn and frayed, when the whole tackle is thrown on one side as worn out, when really three parts of it is as good as ever. As to hooks themselves for barbel, opinions vary; but taking them all in all, I fancy none can beat the good old Carlisle round bends, with a fairly long shank, the best sizes being Nos. 4, 5, 6, 7, and 8, Redditch scale. No. 4 is a useful size for scratchings or tallow cake fishing. Nos. 5 and 6 for worms, No. 7 for the cad-bait, while the No. 8 will come in handy if the angler considers he should like to try a lip hook to his worm tackle. One or two good men that I know in this branch of sport have a decided preference for a double hook, and even a small treble, about perch size, say a No. 9, as a hook for scratching fishing. I have not a word to say against either of them, on the contrary, small doubles and trebles are very useful indeed, especially when the bait is that nice pipey, greasy, luscious bit of tallow cake so beloved of big barbel. If the tyro binds on his own hooks, it behoves him to be very careful in the operation, as the least slackness or carelessness in binding on the silk or fastening off may prove disastrous, and the hook draw away from the gut when subjected to the strong rush of a lively barbel. For binding purposes I prefer good, strong, but fine white or yellow silk. This silk should not be any thicker than, say, a bit of 3x drawn gut. Carc should be taken that it is soft in texture and loosely twisted. I don't like the silk to feel stiff and hard to the fingers. This is the great point, as soft silk can be bound flat to the shank of the hook, and looks almost as if it was part and parcel of the hook itself, so close and neat can it be done. Reels of various coloured silks can be bought at any draper's shop for twopence each; a good deal of this kind is, however, almost too fine, and very little better than floss silk, liable to break at nearly any sort of a pull, so a most careful inspection is necessary. Buttonhole twist is too coarse and stout. Perhaps some of that fine yellow silk that the tailors use in machining or finishing off best goods would be more likely to suit. Years ago I used to get a capital tying silk in Nottingham. It was sold in reels containing 120 yards, and the cost was fivepence. In all probability a similar article can be got nowadays from the draper's in any large town. The next item that the tackle maker requires is a bit of good wax, and I don't mind saying that nothing beats saddler's or shoemaker's wax. For holding, either of them are unrivalled, but unfortunately the colour is black, and presents a strong contrast to a delicately coloured bait like a yellow cad-bait, or even tallow cake, so I am sadly afraid we must pass this wax on one side, and try something else that will be a good substitute, even if it does not stick quite so close. A good colourless wax that I used and recommended twenty years ago can be made for a trifle in this wise:- Two ounces of the best resin, and a quarter of an ounce of beeswax. These can be got for a copper or two at any chemist's. Pound the resin up in small pieces, and cut the beeswax into strips or shavings with a knife; put the two into a strong old breakfast cup, and simmer in the oven for a quarter of an hour or so, or, in fact, till they are quite melted; then add a quarter of an ounce of tallow (a bit from a halfpenny tallow candle will do), and simmer again for another 20 minutes, or until the whole are incorporated, and capable of being poured out of the cup like a thick liquid. This must be done into a large basin of clean, cold water - it will not mix with the water, of course - let is stay there for a minute or two till it cools sufficiently to handle. Lift it out and work with the fingers till perfectly pliable; and, I might add that it is nearly impossible to pull it and work it about too much - 20 minutes, or half an hour even, is none too long for this pulling and working process. At the end of that time it will have a bright and waxy appearance, and can be rolled up into a ball and dropped for several hours into a bucket or other vessel of cold water. When you finally remove it from the water, put it in a tin with a tightly fitting lid, a small coffee tin will do; keep it in a cool place out of the air or sun, and it will keep good for two or three years. Of course, the quantities just given will be too large and awkward to use in the whole, a bit as big as a very small walnut will be ample, and if by any means this wax becomes too hard and brittle to comfortably use, a drop or two of oil worked well among it will rectify that little difficulty. Even in such a little thing as waxing a bit of silk there is, my young friends, a right and a wrong way of doing it. The proper way is to break 14 or 15 inches from your reel of silk, and hold one end tightly between your teeth and the other end between the thumb and forefinger of the left hand, pull tight, now rub the wax a few times up and down the silk - top and bottom - until all is waxed, taking care that no lumps stick to it, or yet too much wax is used. Just a slight coat all over is plenty. Next finish waxing the two ends. Now take up a hook between the thumb and forefinger of the left hand, holding it by the bend, and wind a few turns of the silk tightly round the shank, beginning about midway and finishing close against the end of the shank; the thumbnail of the hand that holds the hook will also hold the end of the silk from slipping. Pick up a length of gut and draw about half an inch of one end between your teeth to flatten it slightly, so that it will hold tightly to the hook, and lay it along the shank on the inside of the hook, that is, towards the bend, and bind the silk tightly and closely round the hook and gut, beginning, of course, at end of shank and finishing off about level with the barb, with two half-hitches over the bend; draw tight, and break the silk close off. The loop at the other end of this length of gut wants binding close and tight in a similar manner. I recommend the binding of this loop to be at least three-quarters of an inch in length. The loop or eye itself need not be larger than a quarter of an inch in diameter. In the preceding chapter I mentioned the plan for making the end of a float red. If the hooks you have just bound on are intended for worm tackle, a little of that red-coloured varnish made thin, and painted carefully over the whipping will be an improvement. It will be about the same colour as a well-scoured worm, beside a good protection to the whipping itself. The other hooks that you bind on for cad-bait and scratchings must be carefully painted with the plain varnish without any colour added.

Another very useful article in the barbel fisherman's outfit is a float and tackle case, and this should be specially made. The tackle books generally sold are not much good for this purpose, at any rate. The usual pattern is a good deal in the shape of a pocket-book, or a fly-book, some 8in long by 4in wide, and 2in thick, with a line winder fitted in a partition in the centre. This kind of tackle case affords no protection to the long floats necessary in barbel fishing. Some of these floats are as much as 10 inches in length, and if by any chance you fitted them in an 8 inch book the ends would stick out, and be liable at any moment to be broken. A case that I strongly recommend can be made by any handy man with a little assistance from a shoemaker or saddler. I will explain its materials and manufacture. Procure from the currier or leather seller's a bit of leather known in the trade as 'grain hide,' it is fairly stout, about as thick, I should say, as the uppers of light boots; it is black in colour and mottled on one side, and brown on the other. The size you will require is 30 inches long by 11 inches in width. Cut the piece exactly to that size, and see that the edges are level and exactly an oblong; that is, as big one end as it is the other, and every corner square. Cut the corners off one end so that it is slightly rounded –

this forms the leaf, or outside flap of the case. Another bit of similar leather is now required 20 inches long and 11 inches wide. This bit should also be cut perfectly level, and every corner square. Divide this last bit into five equal parts, 4 inches wide by 11 inches long. Lay these five pieces level on the other one, one above another, about an inch apart. Six strips of thin leather is the next time, each $4^{1}/_{2}$ inches long by $^{3}/_{4}$ inch wide. These six strips are first of all sewn on the three topmost pieces of leather just referred to; two on each, about two inches from each edge, and about six or seven inches apart. Each of these strips should be subdivided by three rows of stitches, in addition to the two at the top and bottom edges. If this is carefully and accurately done, loops are formed for the reception of the floats, or anything else of a similar character. After these strips are all stitched on, and be sure and put them on the black or outside of the leather, take a little gum and stick the edges of each partition exactly in its place, and enlist the services of a friendly saddler or tailor who has a strong sewing machine, and get him to stitch with strong yellow silk twice right round the edge and across the bottoms of every separate partition or pocket. After this is done another row of stitches right down the centre of the three topmost partitions will make six divisions of them, each about five inches wide by four deep, and will be found very handy for storing away a variety of things, such as loose hooks in envelopes, a few yards of waxed silk - fine and stout - wrapped on a bit of stiff card, a little flat tin box holding a bit of wax, or any other small item that can be stowed away in an envelope. The two partitions at the bottom I recommend to be left the full size open, the bottom one of all to contain a winder for tackle, and the one above it for storing gut hooks in. If these gut hooks are put up in half-dozens, each half dozen being in one of 'Allcock's patent gut hook wrappers,' they can be kept with the gut nearly straight, lying full length in that wide pocket, which will be found much handier, and nothing like so wasteful as if each packet of gut hooks was coiled up in an envelope. The tackle winder just referred to can be made with four thin strips of hard wood, each strip nine inches long, half an inch wide, and one-eighth of an inch thick. These strips of wood can be connected together by four pieces of stout brass wire, say an eighth thick, and three inches long, at regular distances from each other, the whole concern when finished being about three inches wide by nine long, in four partitions, and capable of holding nearly any amount of shotted tackle. The connecting wires should be placed, one within half an inch of each end, and the other two in the centre, about two inches from each other. This is a very strong tackle case, and will last a man, if he is careful, the whole of his life. I might have added that a buckle and strap should be put on the leather case, and when folded up in five folds is then 11 inches long by 5 inches wide, and does not take up very much room in the angler's bag or basket. A dozen long barbel floats, a disgorger, a small pair of scissors, ditto pliers, in addition to the other things named can be stowed away in this case and thrown into the basket without any chance of damaging any of its contents. The total cost of this case would not exceed five or six shillings, not a very serious item when we consider the great usefulness and the lasting qualities of it.

I have just mentioned the basket, and this is another

thing the barbel fisherman must have. He has a variety of articles to carry, probably altogether of some little weight, so he wants one fairly strong, and, above all, roomy. A small French creel, one of those white wicker affairs with a hole in the lid, is no use at all for this purpose. Some anglers go in for a seat basket, and most certainly they are a great improvement on the creel, so far as the requirements of the bottom fisherman are concerned. I like to carry a folding stool to sit on. Perhaps one reason why I don't care to use a basket as a seat is the fact that my weight soon squeezes it out of shape. A pattern that is effected by many of the Trent men is somewhat after the fashion of a carpenter's tool basket, except that it is deeper, and is as wide at top as it is at bottom. A good one is some 30 inches long by 14 or 15 inches deep, and six inches, or even eight inches, across the bottom. Some of these baskets have a partition in them. They are made of mat or fine rushes, bound all round the edges, down the sides, across the bottom, and over the handles with two or three rows of strong webbing. In carrying these baskets to and from the river the landing net shaft is put through the two small handles and hoisted across the shoulder. One of the most useful fishing bags I ever had I bought from a Government contractor, who deals in all sorts of spare and out-of-date stores. It was originally made for a parcel postman, and is wonderfully strong and waterproof, measuring two feet in length by 18 inches deep, and very roomy inside. A strong webbing strap enables it to be carried across the angler's shoulders. I fitted a stout partition in it lengthways, and it is astonishing what can be packed up inside that bag; in fact, I always consider it to be one of the best investments I ever made. If my memory is correct I only paid a matter of four shillings for it. I strongly advise the novice to keep his eyes on the advertisement columns of the newspapers he reads; he may see a similar article for sale, and I know by practical experience that it is one of the most useful things a barbel fisherman can have. Tackle case, reels, cocoa-nut shell, and old scissors for clipping up worms, string, knife, lunch, or dinner, etc., etc., can be carried in one partition of that bag, and in the other can be packed away bags of worms, scratchings, or even ground bait, tins of gentles, or anything else of the kind that the angler considers he should like to take with him.

A good calico bag will be found the best to carry worms or scratchings in, and don't be frightened at having the bag big enough, as a thousand lob-worms, among half a peck of damp moss is no trifle; while as a fish bag nothing will beat a bit of draper's packing material - flax, I think it is called. These materials can be bought for a trifle anywhere. In penning this chapter I have had the pocket of the working man fisherman before me. Everything can be bought or made without any very serious expenditure, and as an old working man angler myself, I know they are every bit as effective as an outfit costing, say, a matter of six or seven pounds, perhaps a good deal more so.

CHAPTER V

HOOK AND GROUND BAITS FOR BARBEL

Barbel in Walton's time - Barbel fare - Cad-bait - Lob-worms - How to collect - How to scour - Leen-worms - Brandling worms - Scratchings, or tallow-cake - Ground-bait for Barbel.

Izaak Walton, when writing of the barbel, uses a very significant passage, he says:- 'The barbel is curious for his baits, that they may be clean and sweet; that is to say, to have your worms well scoured, and not kept in sour or musty moss, for he is a curious feeder; but at a well-scoured lob-worm he will bite as boldly as at any bait, and especially if the night or two before you fish for him you shall bait the places where you intend to fish for him with big worms cut into pieces, and note that none did over-bait the place, or fish too early or too late for a barbel.' When my attention was first directed to the sentences just quoted, they struck me at once as being peculiarly up to date, and remarkably appropriate for even this go-a-head nineteenth century. I thought to myself: now here is a fish that, despite the march of civilisation, despite the vast changes and improvements that have taken place in the angler's baits and appliances, has not changed his character, for to-day he is the same in his tastes as he was 250 years ago, for the words just referred to were penned by our Father Izaak in the seventeenth century, and they are just as appropriate as though they were only written last week. A barbel is 'curious for his baits,' perhaps a little more curious now than he was at that time. He also is 'a curious feeder,' and that with a vengeance; and as for a 'well-scoured lob-worm,' why, it has the same attraction now as it had in Walton's time; and if the instructions then given as to sour moss and clean baits were so necessary, how much more desirable is it to pay particular attention to those items in our time. Barbel can be taken by a variety of baits, such as cad-baits, worms, tallow cake, cheese, gentles, paste, boiled wheat, shrimps, bits of fresh-killed lamprey eels, and in some places, but more particularly down the lower reaches of the Trent, they are regularly fished for with strips of raw, lean beef, and also bits of lean ham. The Gainsborough men are particularly skilful in the use of these last two items. I have given a somewhat formidable list of barbel baits, but the majority of them are only what we can call chance lures - a sort of a forlorn hope when the regular baits fail. The first three named, that is, cad-baits, worms, and tallow cake, are only recognised a the orthodox baits by the general barbel fisherman, and the order of using them can be put as follows:- First, cad-baits, for use during the early part of the season, whilst the fish are on the gravelly shallows after spawning and scouring; then worms during the summer; and, finally, tallow cake during the autumn. Ground-baiting a barbel swim is also a matter of particular moment. A great amount of care must be exercised in this operation, not only in the proper selection of a swim, but also in the quantity of bait put in it. The chief object to be borne in mind is to place before the fish sufficient to entice them to stay in that swim in expectation of more, and if this baiting is done judiciously the occupants of the swim keep working backwards and forwards over the same ground, anxiously looking out for further favours in that direction, whereas if an overdose is given, particularly tallow cake, the fish are apt to be sickened, and utterly refuse even the most tempting tit-bit that can be offered them. I will first of all describe the baits used by the barbeller, giving a few hints as to where to look for them and when, and how to prepare them as I go along.

The cad-bait is the larvæ of some particular sorts of water flies, probably the stone fly, the sedge fly, or some others of a similar nature. It is a curious insect and lives in a house of most wonderful construction. The outside of this dwelling is a good deal like a miniature rockery, and is composed of minute stones, tiny shells, and sand, these component parts being stuck together by some glutinous substance exhuded from the insect itself. The inside of this strange dwelling is smooth and comfortable for the inmate. One of the most curious things about the cad-bait is the places where he is principally found, the wonder being how did he originally get there? For very often a whole colony of them - even as many as 50 - are found sticking on the underside of a big stone, between the said stone and the bottom of the river. The shallower parts of the stream are the places to look for this bait. The men who make it their business to supply anglers with this commodity generally take off stockings and shoes, turn up the trousers to the thigh, and wade in, carefully turning over every stone within reach, most minutely examining the underside of every one, and bagging all baits they can find. These baits are always found under water, and should be searched for where stones, or even old slag, and dross (which are very often used in repairing the river banks) are the most plentiful. Sometimes they are found sticking to old woodwork and submerged roots and boughs. This insect, house, and all is about three-quarters of an inch in length by a quarter of an inch in diameter. The angler will also notice that one end is rounded off, and at the opposite end there is a small opening, from which two or three legs, and just the tip of its head, are protruding. With finger and thumb take hold of this head end, and draw it out of the shell. Some of them are a good deal larger than a maggot, the colour of the best being a brilliant yellow. Others are of a dirty white; others, again, are green; the best for the hook are the yellow ones with a black head. I suppose I need not tell the novice that the outside shell should not be placed upon the hook; the occupant of this shell is only required, you can easily draw it out by the head, and, I might add, as some people are very nervous on the subject of insects, that they are perfectly harmless. Two or three of these cad-baits, carefully threaded on a No. 6 or 7 Carlisle hook, is one of the very best early baits for barbel, say, during the latter end of June and all through July. Most certainly nothing else can beat them for use while those fish are on the shallows. The streams, runs, curly corners, and where the froth keeps churning about on the surface, in the immediate vicinity of the foot of a weir; the gravelly shallows, especially in those portions of the river that are not disturbed by navigation; the shallow streams by the side of old, rotten woodwork, or stick-mended banks; or between the piles and timbers of an old wooden bridge, or even brickwork. All these places are much affected by barbel during the early part of the season, when cad-bait fishing is in full swing. The bait now under notice is the best if used as soon as collected; they speedily turn soft and flabby, soon losing the bright yellow gloss that I fancy is their great attraction. I have tried various dodges to keep them fresh and bright, such as putting them (shells and all, of course) into a vessel of water, and changing the water several times a day, keeping them in damp moss the same as worms. This latter plan did succeed a little, as they kept fairly fresh in moss three or four days; but, speaking generally, they lost their sheen and attractiveness if kept longer than a couple of days, and would soon protrude half their lengths from the shell, grow thin rapidly, and change to a dirty white in colour. The worst feature in using this bait so early in the season is the fact that the barbel caught are apt to be very indifferent in condition.

One of the most important baits in the list of the expert barbeller is worms; and of the many different sorts of worms that exist, three only will concern us now. First and foremost must be put the lob-worm, called by some the dew-worm, the maiden or ringless worm being used on the hook, and the larger and coarser ones as ground bait. Second comes the leen worm, a very lively worm of a deep red colour, and a grand bait for barbel, more especially in very hot, dry weather, when the streams have run down to nearly their lowest level. Third must be put brandlings, of the very largest size and most brilliant in colour. These three are, in my opinion, the barbel fisherman's worms par excellence, and deserve something more than just passing reference. The lob, or dew-worm, is generally picked up by candle or lamp light after a fall of rain. A tennis, cricket, or football ground, where the grass is very short being the best places to look for them; failing these, any meadow, provided the grass is short enough and the soil gravelly or sand, will do. It is said that the very best worms in England are picked up from the Nottingham meadows, in close proximity to the Forest. Worms are procured from the grass during the summer months, say from May round to October; and it is very little good looking for them unless there has been a fall of rain, or an extra heavy dew a very few hours previously. Bright moonlight nights are not favourable for the worm-catcher, neither can a success be scored when a cold east wind and a suspicion of frost is the order. Warm, muggy nights, when darkness covers the face of the earth, and scarcely a star is to be seen, is the best time to select. The worm-catcher's implements consist of an old lantern, a lighted candle, and a small-sized pail. Some men carry both lantern and pail in the left hand, leaving the right free to grab the spoil; others have a strap or stout cord round their necks, with the pail suspended in front of them, so that when stooping down it hangs just free from the ground. I used to favour the latter plan. Two or three handfuls of moss in the pail will be an improvement. When our amateur has selected a favourable night, and arrives at the scene of operations, he must proceed with a good deal of caution, and step about as quietly as possible, for worms sometimes are remarkably sensitive. He holds the lantern in his left hand, in such a position that the rays from the light are flashed along the ground directly in front of him. He may see within the radius of that light perhaps half a dozen worms stretched out along the grass, their tails within their holes, and their heads moving gently about. He makes a move to grab one, when, like a flash, the whole of them vanish as if by magic. This sometimes will happen: certain nights the worms are so very sensitive, there may be plenty out, but the amateur finds himself unable to get even a couple of hundred within two or three hours. Other nights, again, it may be exactly opposite, and the worms can nearly be scraped up, 1,000 or even 2,000 being not unfrequently got in a single outing. In collecting worms they must be grabbed quickly and quietly about an inch or so from the head or free end, and drawn gently from their holes, taking care, however, that they are not nipped or broken. This is a most important point, as bruised worms soon turn bad. If they are seized firmly with finger and thumb and drawn slowly and carefully upwards, avoiding all unnecessary twisting or pinching, the percentage of bruised worms will not be very large. Some of the professional worm-catchers are so expert in the business that they will pick them out of the grass in a twink, and not have half a dozen crushed worms in a thousand. There is one little thing I must, however, caution the novice in, and that is if he can possibly help it, after seizing his worm, he must keep it from drawing its tail further into its hole; if it only succeeds in gaining an inch of ground, ten to one if it can be withdrawn again without pulling in halves. Seize each one firmly, and keep them stretched at full length, and they will soon come out. Some of the worms may look very small, and when stretched out on the grass scarcely thicker than string. It is important that all these should be picked up, as well as the large ones, because the little ones are the famous maiden worms that are so valuable as a hook bait. In some towns, especially in Nottingham, there are certain places that are known as worm farms, where a staff of men are employed to collect the worms, scour them in moss, and when ready pack them up in bags and despatch by train to the various barbel fishing stations on the Thames, Trent, Kennett, and other barbel waters. A very considerable trade is done during the season, but as the price of these worms runs from three to four shillings per 1,000 a working man angler can hardly afford to invest in the quantity requisite to properly bait a barbel swim, so perhaps these few hints, as to how to procure them and prepare for bait, may be useful. After the worms are collected, the next business is to scour them, and even worms used in ground-baiting will be all the better if scoured for two or three days. The dampest corner of a dark cellar is the best place to keep them in; failing that any very cool position where the sun cannot shine on them will do. A wooden vessel is the best to keep and scour them in, and nothing will beat an old beer barrel that is sound and free from holes. This barrel should be cut in half, right round the centre; this makes a couple of capital tubs; if they are well scalded and washed out, all the better. Two or three sound old cheese boxes also make beautiful scouring tubs. The boxes that I mean are those that cheese is packed up in that comes from abroad; each box is round in shape, about two feet across, and 14 inches deep, and made of some light, thin, but strong wood. I know of nothing better to keep worms in. Damp moss, as before hinted, is the best to scour worms in, and this moss should be collected during the latter part of May and the beginning of June. I always fancy it is in the best condition then. The long green moss that grows on the sunny side of an embankment that slopes up to the foot of the hedge is capital stuff; while the stag's horn moss that is found on the grass drives in a wood or forest cannot well be beaten. If the novice lives anywhere handy to a moss-grown wood or meadow, he will do well to collect a good-sized bag full, and spread it out in the sun for a day or two to dry; this moss will then keep green and good for the remainder of the season without troubling to collect fresh every time a new lot of worms wanted scouring. Before using it should be pulled apart, that is, loosened well, and all the bits of sticks, dried grass, and roots picked out; then damp it very slightly, and put a sufficient quantity into two of the tubs. The worms that have already been collected now want separating, the smallest and reddest putting in one tub, and the largest and coarsest in the other. The small worms that have no bands, knobs, or rings on them are the maiden lobs. These worms should be sorted over every day, all damaged ones being carefully thrown out, and as they generally work their way to the bottom of the tub they should be placed as often as possible on the top of the moss again. In about a week they will be fairly well scoured and ready for use. If the weather is very hot and dry during the time the worms are scouring, and the moss feels dry to the touch, a very little drop of water should be lightly sprinkled on the top. The worms that are picked out as hook baits should have plenty of moss with them, and care should be taken that this is kept clean and slightly damp. If this is attended to, the one lot of moss will be quite sufficient to scour the worms, without being at the trouble of changing it. I strongly recommend a fresh supply for every fresh lot of worms, as the used moss will not do very well a second time. The larger worms intended for groundbait should also be examined from time to time, all dead and damaged ones being removed; but these are not so particular as those intended for the hook. By carefully sorting his lob-worms into two separate lots, and looking well after them, the amateur will have well scoured worms lively as crickets, tough as indiarubber nearly, and as red as cherries. I might add that the maiden lobs will live in moss a much longer time than the large coarse ones. I have kept a former in good condition as long as four or five weeks, whereas the others would not last more than eight or nine days at the very outside; but this depends a great deal on the weather, and, above all, on a careful examination of them every day. I should not keep too many worms in each tub, 300 or 400 at the outside of the maiden lobs, and 1,000 of the large ones being plenty; sooner have another box or two than crowd them too thick, if the angler has been lucky enough to get an extra large quantity of them. In any case it is advisable to use the ground bait worms within five or six days at most after picking them up, if the angler can anyhow manage it.

The leen* worm is next in importance; indeed, I have an idea that during certain conditions of weather and water it is the more certain killer of the two. This worm runs from two to four inches in length, and is very lively, and also wonderfully tender. If you are ever so careful in inserting a hook in one, a gaping wound is made from which the white flesh protrudes, and sometimes in handling them, without any apparent reason, they will fall in halves. It is blood red in colour, the tail end is very broad and flat, and the head end is several shades darker than the ordinary

* Similar to the Londoner's Marsh Worm.

lob-worm. The best of them are found in damp corners close to the river's edge. Sometimes a heap of old flood rack that had been swept down the river by a fresh, gets lodged in a quiet corner high and dry. If this is turned over with a fork or a stick, these worms will be found underneath. Some odd times when the blazing sun has been pouring down day after day, and lob-worms could not be procured for either love or money, I have carefully overhauled a heap of this old flood rack, that consisted of rushes, flags, straw, leaves, sticks, and other odds and ends which had probably laid there for weeks unnoticed, and found a good handful of those worms; that in several cases I can call to mind proved a veritable godsend. These worms can be used as soon as collected, but great care must be exercised in putting them on the hook, because of their extreme tenderness. A day or two in moss toughens and improves them. Some of the Trent men consider these worms the very best barbel bait that can be used, and most certainly when the river was running at a very low ebb, and the weather hot and dry, they have proved themselves killers when nothing else succeeded. Once in particular I remember three of us giving a swim nearly opposite Carlton Church, on the Lower Trent, a heavy baiting of lob-worms; but owing to the extreme brightness of the water, sport, particularly among the barbel, was not very brisk. Our total bag at 4 o'clock in the afternoon was three barbel, averaging about as many pounds apiece, in addition to a couple of dozen good roach, dace, and flounders. We had held a council of war, and the opinion of the majority was to the effect that instead of baiting with worms we ought to have given the swim a dose of scratchings, as it was clearly weather and water for the latter bait. A voyage of discovery along the bank led to the finding of about a score leen worms of extra large size; these were tried as a forlorn hope, but before 7 o'clock - the time agreed to pack up - ten more good barbel had gone to swell the bag, besides hooking three or four more that broke away. Another time the late George Wakeland, a noted Trent angler, was fishing close to another equally distinguished barbeller. George used leen worms, the other maiden dews; the former got half a dozen splendid barbel, the latter not a touch, as far as he could ascertain, during the whole of the afternoon. But, on the other hand, I can remember lots of times when even those worms failed to entice a single fish; but still the experiment is worth trying, if the worms now under notice can anyhow be procured. Another worm that is extremely useful as a change bait for barbel is a brandling of the very largest size. I have seen these as large as moderate sized dew worms - over four inches in length, and a corresponding thickness. The very best and biggest that I ever dropped across was in an old rotten tan heap (this is the refuse from the leather tanner's skin yard). I never saw such brandlings before in my life as those; some of them were nearly five inches long, and the alternate rings of red and yellow that is the distinguishing feature of those worms were brilliant in the extreme. They felt to the touch nearly like a strip of tough skin, or perhaps flesh would be a better term. I thought at the time it was most likely the old tan they lived in, that gave them such a clean and brilliant appearance, and such a tough leathery skin.

Sometimes these worms can be found in a heap of old decaying vegetable matter, or in an old manure heap. A hot-bed that has been discarded by the gardener very often contains a large quantity of brandlings; at any rate those are the situations to look for them in ancient manure-heaps and such like places. In the fen district these worms are known as 'spangles'; the brilliant jacket of red and yellow bars they wear no doubt giving them that very appropriate name. There is one thing against these worms, and that is, while fresh, they have an awful disagreeable smell, and a nasty thick yellowish fluid exudes from them at the slightest prick of a hook, which to say the least is not very nice to a sensitive nose. A few days among clean, damp moss, will remedy this drawback somewhat, but this worm if kept too long scouring has a knack of getting smaller by degrees and beautifully less. One old angler used to tell me that it was the smell of a freshly got brandling that was the attraction for Mr. Barbel; at any rate I preferred them scoured a little, but I most certainly do know by practical experience that a large and brilliant brandling is a capital change bait for a barbel. If a dozen Trent barbel fishermen, picked at random, were in a room, and the question: Which is the best bait, worms, or tallow-cake? was discussed and voted upon, I fancy the votes would be pretty nigh equal. Some men of experience swear by worms, while others of equal skill and knowledge favour tallow-cake. Then, again, there are others who, like myself, have no particular choice, but like one bait equally as well as the other. I have heard my friend, Mr. William Ball, the famous 'Trentsider,' of Newark, say more than once that his vote would go unreservedly in favour of tallow-cake, and he is an expert barbeller. Another one of even longer experience once said in my hearing, that if by some chance he was tied to one bait, and not allowed to use any other, and had his own choice, he should say without hesitation, 'give me worms.' In the face of these conflicting opinions it is somewhat difficult to lay down a hard and fast line as to which really is the best; but I fancy the man who is not wedded firmly to any one style, but leaves himself open to try anything that takes his fancy, stands a bit the best chance. This being so, I will now describe how to make an attractive ground bait from tallow-cake, or scratchings. If the reader will turn to Chap. 3 on Chub fishing he will there find a description of Chandler's greaves, scratchings, or tallow-cake, and what it is; but in the case of barbel fishing this bait wants preparing somewhat differently. As recommended for chub this tallow-cake is not much good unless it is of the very best English make; it should be broken in small pieces and boiled in an old saucepan with plenty of water for nearly an hour, being stirred up from time to time with a stick during that process. As soon as it is cooked sufficiently, drain the whole of the water from it, for if allowed to stand in the water the stuff turns black in colour, and disagreeable, which, of all things, must be avoided. The best and whitest pieces of tallow-cake generally rise to the top of the saucepan, and these should be carefully picked out and put in a bag for hook baits, and don't be frightened at picking plenty out; search the mass well over, and remember to select all the whitest, and most luscious-looking bits. The rest of it should be chopped up small, whilst warm, and mixed with a quartern of boiled potatoes, crushed up well, and, say, a half-peck of barley meal, or good fourths. The whole of these ingredients now require incorporating thoroughly, and mixing well together, till it is like a stiff pudding; if too dry, add a little water, and if too soft, another handful of barley meal will rectify it; it should be mixed and worked till it hangs together in a lump; if this is properly attended to the bait will sink to the bottom of the river nearly like a stone. I should say that a sufficient quantity of this ground bait for nearly any swim ought not to be more than a score of balls, each the size of a cricket ball, for this bait, be it noted, must be used very judiciously indeed. A reckless ground-baiting with a whole lot of it day after day, would utterly frustrate the angler's object, and drive the sickened fish out of the swim, instead of hungry ones being enticed into it. My plan would be to bait it little and often, and I don't care to keep scratchings unused above a couple of days. If the angler has plenty of time on his hands he might boil his scratchings and mix his bait at twice, taking care to have the largest lot the first time, and give the swim a gradually decreasing quantity each day for four or five days before he fished it. If, on the other hand, he had only one day to spare, why it would be no choice, but still if he could drop half his bait in on the previous day and the remainder 'little and often' while fishing it would be all the better, but always remember in using scratchings for barbel, if the ground-baiting goes on the same day as fishing, don't overdo it, it must not have half the bait, as if you had a whole week to prepare a swim in. My opinion is that September is the best month for the bait now under review, and it is essentially a low, clear water bait. When the river has run down to its lowest level, and the water is so clear that you can see the bottom, if barbel are to be caught (and Trent barbellers like a low water) then scratchings will be found as cheap and as safe a bait as can be tried.

CHAPTER VI

ON FISHING A BARBEL SWIM

Selecting a swim - Flannel weed - Baiting a swim - The curved float - Casting a bait from the Reel - Fishing a swim - Baiting the hooks - Roving for Barbel - Stret-pegging - Ledgering - Night-fishing - Clay-balling - Barbel in winter.

Anglers who are in the habit of fishing certain waters regularly, soon get to know the characteristics of the various swims; this one, they will say, is a capital barbel swim; all along yon hollow bank the chub most do congregate; that corner is a grand eddy for bream; whilst that quiet swim just beyond the bend is one of the finest places on the whole river for roach and dace. Of course anyone possessed of local knowledge such as that would not have the slightest difficulty in selecting a swim suitable for the sport he had in view. The occasional visitor, and the novice in the art, would have a much more formidable task in properly selecting a suitable swim, and groundbaiting it to the best advantage. I don't know, however, whether it would be altogether an unmixed blessing for the stranger to know the exact whereabouts of the regular barbel swims that have been fished every season for a generation past, and are known to the locals by some recognised name. I always fancied trying fresh water and new swims whenever I had a favourable opportunity, leaving the old places that were nearly fished to death severely alone, and I am not certain but what it paid. I have tried places where I never saw a barbel fisherman at work, and done well in them, not only as regarded the quantity of fish taken, but the size also was much larger on the average; the barbel did not seem so shy, that is the bigger ones, as they did in the constantly fished swims. In some of the preceding chapters I have given advice as to the places where to find barbel during the varied seasons of the year, so I will content myself now by giving just a few general hints. If the angler can find a swim that is moderate in flow, and about eight to ten feet deep, with a gravelly bottom tolerably level, he will do well to cultivate its acquaintance. To find out whether this swim is fairly level or not would be best accomplished by taking a few preliminary swims with float and shotted tackle all down its course, for say, a distance of from twenty to thirty yards, keep shifting the float on the line until you get the exact depth of the water immediately in front of where you stand, and then see if the float will travel fairly and squarely all down the swim, (this will be explained when I come to describe how to fish a barbel swim), then shift your position a few yards lower down stream, and again try the depth, and so on, every few paces, until you have covered the whole of the water that first took your fancy as a swim. If the depth is thereabouts uniform all its length, and no serious obstructions line the bottom, it is a swim that can be fished by float tackle; if, on the other hand, the swim varies greatly in depth, some places being a yard or more deeper than others, it is not so good for the float, at any rate, and a fresh one should be sought out. I used to be very fond of a swim that was not far from a bend in the river, provided there was a proper depth of water, and a pretty fair stream. If we could find a stream with a level bottom in the immediately vicinity of what the Trent men call an umbrella, that is a deep eddying, curling hole, we used to fancy the barbel would be attracted out of the hole into the leveller swim by a judicious baiting. We did not care for the very deepest holes, nor did we favour extra shallow water (unless we were cad-bait fishing during the early part of the season), also we liked the streams that were moderate in flow, avoiding those that galloped away like a mill-race, and also those that were too sluggish. Sometimes the eddies and streams that flow and curl from the foot of a weir, even if the water is no more than four feet deep, contain barbel, very often of the largest size. If the angler can only find a good level swim, that is not far from a very heavy run of water, but a good deal quieter in its own character, good barbel often stay and rest in it when tired of battling with the rapid current close by. Barbel, during the summer months, are constantly on the 'pitch.' One can hardly take a walk for any distance along the river side during July, August, and September, but what we see one or more leap above the surface of the water, turn a summersault, and drop back into the stream with a sounding splash. If that particular place is carefully watched for half-an-hour, in all probability several more will jump, perhaps this will happen all down the length of one meadow. If this occurs, the would-be barbel fisherman should select the easiest run of water in the thick of the 'pitching' fish, carefully take the depth, and ascertain if the bottom is level, and then proceed to bait it up. (They say the reason barbel jump like this is because they are troubled with parasites, and do it to get rid of the nuisance.) One of the worst difficulties the Trent barbeller has to contend with is the great prevalence of flannel weed. In some parts of the river this curious weed covers the bottom like a thick carpet, speedily covering and completely hiding the bait. A carefully swum tackle along the bottom will, however, tell the novice if this weed exists in such a quantity as to render it next to impossible to expect success in that particular place. A friend of mine, when he suspected flannel weed in a swim, used to rig up a ledger tackle, mounted with a couple of small treble hooks, and proceed to find out by raking. He would throw the ledger out across the swim, and allow it to sink to the bottom, and then wind it slowly back again to the bank, repeating this operation carefully every few yards. If this weed existed in any great quantity, the hooks would soon discover it, and the swim could be rejected. If, on the other hand, this weed was only in little patches, why, it would not matter so much. These little matters, such as trying the bottom for depth, levelness of swim, obstructions, and flannel weed on the bottom, should be attended to by the stranger, before he throws any ground bait in. It won't take him long with the help of his rod, reel, line, and tackle, and may save him some considerable trouble afterwards. Having now selected a swim, we proceed to bait it up, and here again some considerable judgement is required. In the first place, the set of the stream must be taken into account; sometimes the water runs in the direction of the bank on which you stand, and sometimes it flows to the opposite shore; in some cases, if the ground bait is thrown four or five yards from the bank, by the time it reaches the bottom it may be fifteen or twenty yards wide; then, on the other hand, it may come towards the shore and lodge within a yard or two of the bank. The best plan is to take a few bits of dried stick, throw them on the water, and watch which way they float; by this means the exact distance to cast the ground bait, so that it is distributed on the bottom of the river exactly where it is convenient for the hook bait to travel can be hit to a nicety. Then, again, the strength of the current must not be overlooked. It is just possible the novice may scatter in his worms, and by such time as they reach the bottom his hook bait does not reach them within several yards. A careful calculation should be made on this point. Sometimes he will find it necessary to walk as many as fifteen or twenty yards higher up stream than where he stands in order to be exactly right, and at other places he need not be more than four or five, or even exactly opposite where he stands. We will suppose the angler can only spare one day for barbel fishing at a time, and he reaches the scene of operations in the early morning, and wants to ground-bait to the best advantage for that day only. He perhaps knows of, and has selected in his own mind, a good swim beforehand. He will want six or seven hundred large lob-worms in one bag for ground bait, and, say, a hundred beautifully scoured maiden worms for the hook in another bag - that is, if worms are his selection. If he knows his ground before he puts his tackle together, he clips up with an old pair of scissors, and the half of a coconut shell, some two hundred of the largest and coarsest worms he has got, and throws them in. This first dose of worms should be cut up into pieces about an inch in length; about an hour afterwards another hundred should be given them, clipped up in a similar manner to the first, and after that twenty at a time only, repeating this several times an hour during the earlier hours of the day, taking care, however that these little lots of worms are cut up small, say in pieces not exceeding half an inch in length. When ground-baiting for barbel on the same day as fishing, without previously feeding the swim, I most certainly prefer to do it by little and often, and like the worms cut up as small as possible, particularly during the later stages of the day's fishing. A great quantity of bait under circumstances such as that will be found a mistake. The novice should remember his object is to entice them, and not to gorge the fish clean up within the first two or three hours. He may catch one or two by mistake first off, while they are gorging themselves on the large quantity of bait thrown hastily in, whereas if he does it judiciously by little and often, the barbel may come on and repay him well during the afternoon and evening.

If the angler has time enough on his hands, or lives within easy hail of his barbel swim, he should, if anyhow possible, bait it up for several days before fishing; and if worms are his bait, I say do it at sunrise, or as soon after as possible every morning. All sorts of nocturnal and predatory fish, chiefly eels and the like, are prowling about during the darkness of the night, and would hold high carnival on the baiting of worms if thrown in at sunset, and the barbel would not get their fair share, whereas if the baiting is done at sunrise the nocturnal fish have crawled into their holes or haunts, and the baiting stands a much better chance of accomplishing its object during the day. We will suppose the angler has some fifteen hundred worms for his swim, which number, I might say, is none too many, he takes seven hundred the first morning and throws in. Some barbellers say this first lot should be cast in whole, because they live longer, and are more attractive than if cut up. Now this is a point that I can hardly decide about. I most certainly at one time did do so, and at other times I fancied they were better if cut in halves. Perhaps, taking it on the whole, it would be better to just slice them in two or three pieces, and no more; but the angler can please himself as to whether he cuts up the first lot, or throws them in whole. The next morning he takes down three hundred, and slices them up in a similar manner and throws in. The third morning two hundred can be given, and the fourth one hundred only. The swim can be fished then or the next day. It will be noticed that there are still two hundred coarse worms that I have not accounted for in this baiting; these are for use during fishing, a very few at a time clipped up small and cast in from time to time in the track of the float will serve as gentle reminders to the barbel, and make them feel, as it were, 'at home.' The same rule applies to scratchings - the ground bait described in the last chapter. It must be thrown in under the same rule; in fact, my own opinion is that this bait should be given even more by degrees than worms. The barbel want educating to it gradually; the largest quantity should be given the first time, and then reducing it every day for at least a week, until the last time, when a couple of balls the size of small oranges, will be ample. This ground bait should be thrown in in lumps about the size of hen's eggs; and unless careful tactics are employed it is likely to swim away down the stream some considerable distance before reaching the bottom. The best plan to adopt is to squeeze each little lump firmly and hard together, and hold it for a few seconds in your hand under the water, and then throw it gently a little above the head of the swim. It will be noticed that now the bait begins to sink immediately, and is very quickly out of sight. This is a ground bait that I fancy soon spoils a barbel swim, and if the novice is so foolish as to cross-bait it - that is, throw a lot of scratchings in one day, and a baiting of worms in the next - why, his chance of sport will be very small indeed. The angler should carefully note what I say about this bait in the closing sentences of the last chapter.

Barbel fishing from a boat is much easier than from the bank, and the manner of mooring this craft seems to me to vary on the several waters that this sport is indulged in. In some places the boat or punt is fixed within two or three yards from the bank, and the anglers fish over the side directly above the pitch. On the Trent, where the stream is stronger, the above plan would not succeed very well, the boat in this case being moored further out lengthways down the stream, and directly in the track of the swim, the angler fishing from the end of it, and dropping the ground bait overboard, the swim itself not commencing until at least twenty yards of water had been covered. This intervening distance between the boat and the swim proper is allowed for the ground bait to reach the bottom. In an extra heavy stream we sighed years ago for something that we could let the ground bait in, down to the bottom of the river directly at the stern of the boat, and at first we tried an old net, putting a good handful or two of worms among some clay in it, and sinking the lot overboard, withdrawing it when we thought the action of the water had washed them all out; but this was a tedious job. After a good many experiments my old friend Mr. T. Sunman, a Trent angler of wide experience, succeeded in making a capital concern out of an old corned-beef tin, which proved most useful in ground-baiting a heavy stream from a boat. The bottom of this tin was weighted with about a pound of lead. We used to put the clipped worms, or the tallow cake, whichever bait we happened to be using, in this tin, and lower it carefully to the bottom of the river by means of two cords, one fastened to the bottom, the other to the lid. As soon as the holder reached the bottom, a careful jerking of the cord on the bottom end tipped it upside down, the wire that held the lid lightly in its place would slip off, and the bait slide out. By this means we were able to get fish much nearer the boat, and ground-bait our swim much more compactly, because, do what we would, in a heavy stream, when bait is thrown loosely in from the hand, it straggles about and covers a wide expanse of river bottom. This tin is no use except from a boat. I might add that some years after Mr. Sunman made his famous ground-baiter a Russian nobleman invented a conical-shaped one, of much more general utility, and it is now made and sold by a well-known firm at the very low price of eighteenpence. All barbel fishermen who fish from a punt or boat in very heavy waters most certainly ought to possess one. In barbel fishing with float tackle it ought to be a recognised rule that this float should be no bigger or heavier than the strength of the stream and the depth of the water warrants. The No. 2 pelican quill, or the No. 3 cork float that are described in a previous chapter are plenty for almost any ordinary swim, and here I might point out the peculiarity of the Trent man's curved float. Some of the cork floats used by these anglers are bent very much, and the novice might wonder why this extraordinary shape. When a straight float, that is a cork float with a porcupine quill through the centre, is swimming down a stream, and the water curls and eddies about, this float is liable to twist round and round in the water, and communicates this twist, kink, or curl to the line and tackle, thus hindering the free and even run of the baited hook. When this bent float is put on the line care should be taken that it is fastened by the cap at the top end, and the line threaded through the small ring at the bottom end, so that this line is on the hollow side of the float. Some of these floats are bent so much that when the line is pulled tight there is a space of nearly half an inch between the cork on the centre of the float and the line itself. The object of the curved float will now be apparent to anybody; when swimming down the stream the back of the float goes first, the hollow side being nearest the angler, and when it is held slightly back during its passage down, of course it is next to impossible for this float to spin or twist round. And so it is with a swan quill or a pelican quill; if these floats are bent a little they are all the better for fishing down a stream for either barbel or chub.

I have given instructions elsewhere on the subject of properly shotting a tackle (see the chapter on winter chubbing), and those remarks hold good in respect to barbel fishing. We will suppose the angler is about to fish a swim that he has carefully baited up beforehand according to instructions already given; the first thing he does before putting his rod and tackle together is to clip up very small a dozen large worms and scatter down the swim, or a few little bits of scratchings, according as to which of the two baits he has baited the swim with. Of course, if the operator has carefully followed the instructions, he already knows the exact depth of the place, or can get it very easily. To throw out the bait properly, if the distance is not very far, he simply takes hold of the line between the two first rings on the rod, and draws down a double length or loop of line, and then with a smart forward movement of the rod point, casts the float and tackle out to is destination, exactly in the same manner as described most carefully in the chapter on 'Stream fishing for roach.' Sometimes he may want to cast out an extra long distance; owing to the shallowness of the water for some considerable space the swim may be directly down the centre of the channel. If, under these circumstances, the swim is over eight feet deep, I advise the No. 6 slider cork float to be used, as there directed; if under eight feet use the No. 4 float, and cast the bait out direct from the reel a good deal like throwing out a pike bait. To make this cast wind the float up to the top ring on the rod, and hold the rod in the hollow between the thumb and forefinger of the left hand, with the fingers of that hand clasping the back of the reel, and one of those fingers reaching over to the top edge of the revolving barrel on purpose to act as a skid or brake to stop the revolutions of the easy running reel at the proper moment. The right hand grasps the rod about eight or nine inches above the top ring of the winch fittings, the handles of the reel pointing to the right of the angler; press the second finger of the left hand on the edge of the revolving portion of the reel. After seeing that the float, tackle, and bait hangs free from the point of the rod, you face exactly the place on the water where you want the float to drop, and swing the rod point to your right hand side and partly behind you, then with a smart, but not jerking, swing forward you bring the rod over the water. As soon as the bait and float swings forward you release the reel by taking off the pressure of your finger on the revolving front rim. As soon as the float drops on the water the finger is again pressed tight on the edge of the reel, so as to effectually stop any further revolutions; and this should be done instantly, because if the reel only runs for a second or two after the bait is in the water a tangle of line round the handles may result. Still keeping hold of the rod with the left hand close at the top of the reel as already described, you drop the butt end of the rod into the hollow of the left thigh and lightly press it there, and at the same time leave go of the rod with the right hand, which hand is brought down, and with finger and thumb take hold of the line just where it leaves the reel, on purpose to pay out this line as fast, or nearly so, as the stream requires. It is the best to hold the float slightly back, but not too much so, just enough to keep a tight line during its passage down the swim will do. As soon as the float and bait have travelled the entire distance down stream where you suppose the ground bait to be distributed, hold the float for a very few seconds as stationary as the stream permits, and then strike smartly, but not too heavily. Sometimes at the extreme end of a swim a fish may take hold, so I always prefer to wait a second or two then and strike on the off chance at the end of every swim. Failing to get a bite all down its course, the float is wound back again to the rod point by winding in the line with the reel handles, and the cast and swim repeated. If at anytime during the progress of the float down stream it should draw under water, strike at once, it may be a fish, or it may be only the hook catching on the bottom; never mind, always strike on the disappearance of the float. A good deal of water can be covered by this method, as it is possible to cast a heavy float tackle direct from the reel thirty yards across the water - expert throwers will considerably exceed this - but twenty-five to thirty yards is very good casting indeed. Any distance between that and ten yards can be tried; the bait then travels down stream in several different tracks, thus standing a better chance of finding a feeding barbel on the prowl. In making up the tackle for this heavy float fishing, I prefer, in addition to the split shots on it, a long corking lead; this lead is used more particularly in tight corking, but it is a very useful addition to the tackle now under notice. This lead is about an inch or so long, and about as thick as a goose quill, with a hole lengthways through the centre. This hole should be large enough to allow the knots of the tackle to pass through. Some anglers who only use a short tackle for barbel put this lead on the line, so that it drops down to the loop of the tackle. I prefer it on the gut line itself, say about two and a half feet from the hook. A couple of shots six or seven inches apart - one each side of this lead - keeps it in its proper position. Four or five shots below this lead, and three or four above it, distributed at intervals, makes a capitally weighted tackle for fishing down these heavy streams, and casting with direct from the reel. This is barbel fishing with a travelling or swimming float down a heavy run of water.

Just a word or two now on the subject of baiting the hook. If the water was very clear I found a small bait and a smaller hook than usual the best, a No. 7 or 6 at the outside being ample, and for bait about $1^1/_2$ inches from the tail end of the brightest and reddest maiden worm I could find; thread the hook point in at the broken end and work it up the shank, bring the point and barb out again about a quarter of an inch from the tail end, and thread crossways on the point and barb another very small leen worm for choice, if you can anyhow get them. This is a wonderfully attractive and lively bait, and should be tried for barbel whenever convenient. Another good bait is a single medium-sized maiden lob-worm on a No. 4 or 5 hook; roll this worm among the sand, or dip him in a bag of saw-dust - this helps you to hold him while baiting - run the point of the hook in at the extreme head end, and work the worm up the shank and gut, taking particular care that the hook does not protrude any oftener than you can help. When the point gets about half an inch from the end of the tail bring it out, and then carefully pass it back again till the point of the hook is once more covered. I fancy this keeps the worm in its place, and prevents it from wriggling half its length free from the hook. Sometimes we threaded the worm on in an opposite direction, that is, the tail end up the shank, and the head end downwards. More than once this dodge has scored. Other barbel fishermen again like a lip-hook on the tackle, that is, a smaller one, say a No. 8 firmly whipped on the gut about an inch and a half above the shank of the other one, and most certainly this hook is very useful in holding the worm well up; also it is useful if the angler wants two worms at once as a bait. To bait this the first worm is threaded up the hook and gut as far as the lip-hook; only half an inch of the head end, and about an inch of the tail end should wriggle free. Now take another worm, somewhat smaller than the last, and hang one end of it firmly on the lip-hoop, and the other end on the bottom hook, the point and barb of which are brought out of the first worm for the purpose. This is a capital bait for barbel, there being four ends to twist and wriggle about in a very attractive manner. In baiting a hook with scratchings, as already hinted, the whitest pieces should be used, and these pieces, of course, should be threaded on the shank until you get a lump nearly as big as your thumb end. This bait is swum down the stream with the same tackle and in the same manner as worms.

Another plan of trying for barbel is by roving after them, and for this any of the baits I have mentioned will do. The angler tries any and every likely looking swim that takes his fancy, throwing in a little bait as he goes along, stopping nowhere very long together, unless unexpected luck is met with. Some odd times a very good bag of barbel is made by this means without any previous baiting; but, taking it on the whole, sport cannot be expected to be so good as in a properly baited up-swim.

Still another method adopted by many of the best barbel fishermen is what is known on the Trent as 'stret-pegging,' 'stretting,' and sometimes plain 'pegging.' In other waters this style is known as 'long-corking,' and also 'tight-corking.' For this plan the heavy No. 4 cork float is used, and the tackle with the long-corking lead in the centre, exactly the same as described in fishing a heavy stream; but in this case there can be a couple of shots extra on the gut line.

Swims, or rather eddies, where this plan can be adopted will be the best if very near the bank on which the angler sits or stands, a deepish hole close under an overhanging bank, where there is a shelf under water, or where a stream hits hard under the bank at the bend, and then flows outward again, leaving a curl or eddy on the inside. Sometimes in places like those there is a considerable depth of water, even as many as ten or twelve feet. These are capital places to stret-peg in; in fact, it is the best performed where the curl or hole can be reached with the point of the rod. This class of swim is ground-baited in the same manner as before described - with a dose of worms or scratchings, which ever is the most convenient, great care being taken that this bait is thrown in so that it is swept fair and square into the hole. A little observation will soon enable the angler to hit this to a nicety. The float in this case should be fixed on the line so that it is at least two feet further from the bait than the swim is deep, that is, if the hole is nine feet deep, fix the float at least eleven feet from the bait. Sit on the bank as low down and as close as possible, and just toss the float and bait in front of you, and let it go down the stream on the outer edge of the eddy until it reaches the curl or hole, then hold the float as near stationary as you can; the action of the water will work the bait about on the bottom, and the slightest pull of a barbel will be at once communicated to the float. If the angler can anyhow manage it, he should sit on the bank so that his float is at least ten yards below him, and allowing it to drop down stream a foot every now and then, until the bait has searched the whole of the eddy. In several places, such as I have described, the angler will notice a very heavy stream on the outside of the hole, while a little inside, nearer the bank, the stream is nothing like so strong. In stret-pegging the float should be held tight at first, as close to the inside of the strong stream as possible; by degrees it will work nearer and nearer the bank; when too near, wind it back again and make a fresh cast. Stret-pegging, it should be remembered, is holding the float against the stream as near stationary as the swim permits where the hole operated on is very near the bank. The hook bait and the manner of baiting is exactly the same as for stream fishing.

The ledger is also a capital piece of tackle on which to attempt the capture of barbel; indeed, some anglers say it is the only plan worth trying, because, as they remark with a little reason in the argument, the bait in the first place is sure to be on the bottom, no matter how irregular and uneven the bottom may be; and, second, the work and the exertion required is nothing like so hard as swimming a stream all day with float tackle. Well, there is something to be said in favour of this opinion; but still, personally, work or no work, I prefer the float tackle wherever it can comfortably be adopted, falling back upon the ledger if the swim actually requires operating upon by that particular plan. Sometimes there is a hole a good distance from the bank, the intervening water may be broken and shallow, and the angler sees barbel jump from that hole. It is next to impossible to get a float tackle in it, and if got there would not properly work. Or, again, take an eddy under the boiling, rushing waters of a weir hole, a float would be sucked out of sight and completely drowned in less than no time. The ledger is the tackle for use under those circumstances. The way to make one is this: take two feet of stoutish gut, with a hook at one end and a loop at the other, next a bit of the finest gimp that is made - a foot long or so, with a loop on either end - on this gimp a running bullet is fixed, one about five-eighths of an inch in diameter, with a drilled hole through the centre, then another foot or fifteen inches of stout gut; join these three sections of tackle together by the loops in the usual manner, the longest bit of gut at the bottom, the gimp and bullet in the centre, and the short length of gut at the top; pinch a fair-sized shot on each end of the gimp, close to the whipped loops, so that the bullet has that much play and no more; four or five more split shot of good size can be pinched on the gut immediately below the gimp, and a couple on the bit above it - this is my plan of a ledger. Some anglers simply have a stout gut hook with the lead fixed by the help of half a match on the silk line itself, this lead being the triangular shaped flat one called by the Trent men a 'plumb.' Other anglers recommend the ledger to be one of the very heaviest long pike leads, fastened to the main gut line with a three inch length of very fine gut dangling free as it were, because they say if this lead catches under a stone, or gets immovably fixed in an old snag, the fine gut would break, and nothing be lost except the lead itself. Now I tried that dodge, and at first sight it looked beautiful - in theory - but not much good in actual practice, particularly in very heavy water, because when the ledger was rolling down the stream the fine gut on the lead and the main gut line sometimes twisted tight together, and was very little better than the old-fashioned plan. There appears to me to be three separate and distinct methods of plumbing or ledgering a barbel swim; - first, down a strong stream with a sandy bottom; where the ledger travels at a fair pace; or, should I say, rolls along the bottom of the river, twenty, thirty, or even forty yards, nearly as fast as a float tackle would go. For this plan, the ledger is thrown slightly up stream, and allowed to go down of its own sweet will; of course, jerking it loose with the rod point, if it happens to catch anywhere during its passage; withdrawing, or winding it back again at the end of every swim, and repeating the cast, keeping the lead and bait constantly on the move. Second - ledgering with a 'lodge' bait, that is, thrown down stream into a hole or eddy, and held there as stationary as can be. Third - ledgering from a boat; the boat being moored in a line with the swim, and some twenty or more yards above it; the bait being thrown to the required distance straight down stream; the rod is then laid across the seat with the tip pointing over the stern, in the same direction as the swim runs, winding up every now and again to examine the bait, and make a fresh cast, sometimes nearer the boat, sometimes further away, as occasion requires. I might as well add, that of course no float is used in ledgering; the angler relying upon the feel, or the bobbing of the rod top, to tell him when he gets a bite. The ledger tackle is thrown direct from the reel, (the lead and shots being sufficient weights for this); in exactly the same manner as described in this chapter for throwing a heavy float out. Baits for ledgering are the same as for the other styles of barbel fishing, except that I might say, some anglers swear by the ledger and tallow cake; maintaining that it is the best of all baits to use on a ledger; but it all depends on the state of the weather and water; worms being the best on certain occasions, which occasions I have already indicated. Almost any of the baits that I recommend in the chapter on chub fishing; (that is, bottom baits); will do very well for barbel, as a change, such as a bunch of wasp grubs; a nubble of cheese, or cheese paste; a dozen or so unscoured and stinking gentles, threaded on the hook; and at odd times he will take a large-sized peeled shrimp (the fishmonger's shrimp bear in mind). Sometimes during very hot and dry weather it is nearly useless to fish for barbel during the day time; our knowing angler is just setting out for his sport when the ordinary fisherman is thinking of packing up. At these times he clips up his scratchings as fine as can be; or else, if the swim is too heavy for that, pinches his tallow cake groundbait into little hard balls, not much bigger than his ledger lead; drops a few in well above his pitch, and ledgers until very nearly midnight, using as a hook bait some carefully selected freshly boiled tallow cake, that had been already sorted out in a bag ready for use. If the swim has had a previous baiting all the better; I have known some good specimen barbel to be taken under cover of darkness, or rather, semi-darkness, by this plan, in the very swim that another angler, an hour or two previously, had given up in despair. In some of the quieter parts of the Thames, where the barbel swim is just over the boats' side, the fishermen very often adopt a plan which they call clay-balling; for this, they have a lump of clay and bran mixed up and worked together into a very stiff mass; the bait for the hook is, I think, tallow-cake, or perhaps a bunch of gentles; the clay ball is fixed on the gut line, some couple of inches above the hook. In the middle of this clay ball, a dozen coarse gentles, or a few little bits of tallow-cake are enclosed, the action of the water gradually works these out; Mr. Barbel, if prowling around, picks them up, and maybe at the same time appropriates to his own use the bait on the hook. The clay and bran ball is kept in its position on the gut line by the aid of a little bit of stick, which is fastened securely a few inches from the hook; the spare gut line between hook and clay being just wound round the latter; so that the hook bait itself lays as it were on the side, or at any rate close against the ball. Sometimes a light ledger lead, and two or three split shot, fixed about eighteen inches above the clay ball is used; at other times, the stret-pegging float and tackle is employed; but the method cannot very well be adopted unless the hole or swim is close under the rod point. The plan appears to be a favourite with certain Thames men, when the water is clear and the fish are biting very shy. I might add that this clay ball when first put on the tackle is about the size of a very small hen's egg, and soon shakes free when a barbel takes the bait and is struck.

It is generally accepted as a fact that barbel are a summer fish, going into retirement and a state of torpor as soon as the first frosts of winter come on; now and again we are startled by the announcement that some angler had captured one when chub fishing with pith and brains during the sharp winter; this is set down to chance or an accident, but the fact of the barbel taking bait, and being hooked in the mouth goes to prove that sometimes, even in winter, they feed; perhaps the reason why more are not caught then, is because they are never, or hardly ever, properly fished for. I once heard an old professional fisherman say that he had caught barbel in every month of the year except one; and if I recollect aright the month was February (this old angler's exploits took place before the 'Mundella' Act was thought about). The bait he used was pieces of that very curious fish the lamprey; these eel like fish run during cold weather, and are caught in baskets, sometimes to the tune of hundreds in a day and night; this old angler used to cut about three quarters of an inch from the middle of a lamprey; fresh and bleeding; fix it on a hook, and ledger in the deepest and quietest holes. I have been assured by independent witnesses that very heavy barbel have been killed by that man; even as many as three or four during a single afternoon late in November; and once in particular he had good and unexpected sport even late in December. To speak for myself, I found it a very uncertain business to catch barbel at Christmas time, or even for a few weeks before that; on the very few occasions that I did have a try. Even during the summer season I never could once boast of phenomenal luck; true, I did as well as anybody else under the same conditions, getting very fair bags at times; but then look at the hundreds of hours, one time or another, I have put in at it; so I must again say, and conclude with a warning to the anxious novice, don't expect sport every time you go barbel fishing, they are 'kittle cattle.'

PART II

THE CHUB

CHAPTER I

CHARACTERISTICS OF THE CHUB

Chub Fishing, a retrospect - Trent Chub - Ouse Chub - Weight of Chub - Names of Chub - Habits of Chub - Chub fare - Dace v. small Chub - Superstition in Chub Fishermen.

'The Chub, whose neater name which some a Chevin call.'

This very shy, but sportive, fish has long been the choice object of the coarse fisherman's quest, for there is no other denizen of our rivers and streams that can be captured by a greater variety of baits, or by a greater variety of ways, or in a greater diversity of weather surroundings, than our leather-mouthed friend the chub. Years ago I can remember these fish being among the most plentiful in the waters I then plied my craft in, and older anglers still have told me that, in their youthful days, this characteristic was more marked still. Does not Michael Drayton, the poet, when writing three hundred years ago of the Trent and its fish, say of the chub, 'food to the tyrant pike, most being in his power, who for their numerous store he most doth them devour!' The words 'numerous store' used by the old poet seems to prove that he, at any rate, had noticed the great quantity, that perhaps swarmed down every swim and reach of the river referred to in his day; but as the years roll on, the 'numerous store' seems to be slowly but surely vanishing (from public waters at any rate), and it is only by a minute knowledge of the fish and its haunts during the varying seasons, that a respectable catch can be made, and, alas! that I should say so, good catches of chub from public waters are getting few and far between. When I say good catches, I mean as it was in the good old days of thirty years ago, when a hundredweight of those fish in one day, on a single rod, was not a very uncommon occurrence.

Chub are found in a good many of the streams and rivers of England; very seldom is he an inhabitant of a quiet lake or drain. In some streams where he is not specially fished for, he is apt to get over plentiful, and a bit of a nuisance. Certain trout waters that I know of have more of those fish than they can comfortably maintain, and the result is, when our trout fisher is intent on nobler game, and expecting nothing less, when in conflict with a big fish, than the trout of the season, he finds, to his great disgust, that it is only a huge chub, sport giving and lively enough in all conscience, and a fish that in a coarse fishing water would fill with delight the heart of any ordinary bottom fisherman; but in the case of our trout fisherman I am sadly afraid he causes more strong language than is actually good for the peace of mind of that disappointed angler.

Chub appears to me to depend upon a variety of circumstances for their well-being; they get into the best of condition and reach the greatest weight in streams where they are the least disturbed by navigation, and where heavy and tremendous floods are the least frequent. In the Trent I found, after many years' experience, that very large and splendidly-conditioned chub were only occasionally got, the majority of the fish were long and thin, and presented an appearance as if they had to battle very hard for their existence, constantly harried, as the saying is, from pillar to post; swept from one stream to another by a succession of heavy floods; washed out of their haunts under the banks and boughs by the steamers and the navigation, to say nothing of the constant dredging that is going on to keep the channel clear; all these causes, and perhaps several others combined, help to keep the chub down in the most public parts of the stream; it is only by fishing the quieter runs, and the streams and places that are not so much affected by the causes just noted that decent sport can be relied on. I am aware that now and again good bags can be obtained, but as far as the Trent is concerned, the sport with this fish gets worse every year, and a great alteration will have to take place before it can be anything like the character of bygone days. On the other hand, I find that the chub of the Bedfordshire Ouse are the very best that it has been my good fortune to meet with on any river that I have fished. In certain of the streams and backwaters of that river they are to be met with in very fair numbers; being very little disturbed by either floods or navigation, and still less by anglers, netters, or night-liners; and they are chub! none of your long, lanky fish, all head and jaws, but short, thick, and fat specimens, which, when hooked, fight like demons; and as weed beds, rushes, flags, boughs, and old roots are very plentiful in the immediate neighbourhood of their haunts, they not infrequently proved the victors in the short and sharp struggle that ensued.

I should not like to commit myself as to how big or what weight the chub will reach in these waters of the Ouse district, but in certain places the surrounding conditions of water, food, and natural cover are so pre-eminently suited to them, that I should be safe in stating that, as far as English chub are concerned, the very highest weight of these fish can be attained by them there. I remember once seeing, within the last three or four years, by the side of this river, the head and bones of a giant chub, evidently the remains of a meal left by an otter and the crows, and when I closely scrutinised the massive head, the thickness of the back-bone, the great breadth and length of the tail and fins, the long and strong rib bones, and the tremendous scales lying around, I estimated that he must have weighed, at the very least, 8lb, and it was an unmistakable chub, as the head was hardly touched, and was quite fresh. I have seen and weighed them when they have reached six and a quarter pounds, and odd ones I have observed basking under the cover of the boughs, just below the surface, that have been veritable giants of their race. One of the largest that I ever saw, was taken out of the river Ouse, during a flush of coloured water, with a lob-worm for a bait, and on a gimp ledger tackle; I did not see the fish weighed, but the captor assured me that it went within a trifle of seven pounds, and I did not doubt it. Some very large chub are taken out of this river occasionally when pike fishing, more especially if the water is slightly clouded, and the bait a nice, lively gudgeon; two or three times I have also taken them on a spoon bait, when spinning the runs for jack.

One September afternoon, about four or five years ago, I took with a Zulu fly, four out of one shoal that weighed a little over 17lb, biggest 4lb 7oz; every one of the four was over 4lb, and I was then smashed up by the fifth I hooked - a regular 'growser,' that broke a very stout gut cast as easily as a bit of burnt thread. I shall never forget the leap and splash that chub made when he broke me, and then like shadows the rest of the shoal vanished, and I saw them no more that afternoon. I might go on multiplying these cases, but I think I have said enough to show that the chub of the Ouse are splendid specimens. With regard to the Trent, my top weight during a chub fishing experience that reached to nearly a quarter of a century was a fish that did not reach 6lb by the same number of ounces. The very largest that I ever saw taken from that river was just an ounce over 6lb. I have also had some good bags of chub one time or another from the more streamy parts of the Witham, but I cannot remember a single specimen that ever exceeded 4lb from that river.

Thirty years ago I knew an old angler and collector that used to fix the weight of chub, before he thought them worthy of a glass case, at 6lb, but nowadays, from public waters, at any rate, the angler collector may well be satisfied if he gets one that exceeds, or even reaches, 4½lb, and even they are not got every day; and instead of catching a hundred-weight big and little in one day - that has been done more than once in bygone times - he will have to be satisfied with a dozen fish, ranging from 3lb down to 1½lb each, and even this he will find to be a very exceptional case. When chub used to swarm down every reach and swim of the Trent, anglers thought nothing of taking three or four four-pounders out of one hole; but nowadays, when we hear of such a thing, we set it down to a bit of extra good luck. As recently as January, 1896, there is a report of four chub being sent to Cooper's, of London, for preservation, that went on the aggregate nearly 19lb, and these were taken on one afternoon, and out of one hole, by fair and square angling; so, in the face of evidence like this, I must say to the young angler, 'stick to it, you may create a record one of these days.'

The chub is another distinguished member of the carp tribe, and is known to naturalists by the specific name of Cyprinus Cephalus, which latter of the two has been given to him on account of the size of his head; but really this must be objected to, as the head of a chub, when the fish is in good condition, is not by any means out of proportion to his body. Even the good and gentle Izaak Walton, who loved every living creature, says of him, 'Oh, it is a great logger-headed chub,' and this name has crept down to more modern times. In some districts of England the chub is known as 'the large-headed dace.' In Scotland he is very often called 'a skelly'; the Welsh anglers know him as 'a penci'; and in Sweden, among the boatmen there, he rejoices in the title of 'kubb.' All these names seem to point to the head of the fish, and as a natural result he is branded with a title that he does not deserve. Just look at a real good specimen of three or four pounds, as it lays broadside on a dish, or the grass, and a single glance is sufficient to stamp the term 'loggerhead' as a libel of the most pronounced type. Personally, I call him a very handsome fish, and as a sporting fish in all weathers he has not his equal among the so-called coarse fishes. The very worst that can be said of him is that when you look at him straight in the face he is somewhat coarse looking, and has rather a large mouth. True, he is not much good when you come to cook him, being very bony, watery, and very flavourless. If the angler should, however, like to cook one it can be prepared in the same way as recommended for barbel. Chub spawn during the month of May, and deposit the ova on the gravel in very shallow water; and this occupation is supposed to last about ten or twelve days. During this period, or, perhaps, a week or two later, the chub get perfectly reckless, and will take freely any sort of a bait that is thrown to them. Before the 'Mundella' Act came into force, certain anglers would take advantage of this peculiarity of the unfortunate fish, and haul them out to the tune of scores every day. Any sort of a rough fly that had the hook well garnished with cad-baits or gentles would do when the 'milk,' as we used to call it, was dripping from the captured chub; but the Act just quoted has rectified that little error; the great majority of the fish have left the spawning beds for their summer quarters before the opening day in June.

Chub are a wonderfully shy fish; I should say, without exception, they are the shyest that swim - of course the few days referred to in the preceding paragraph must not be taken into account. When they take up their quarters in their regular homes and haunts they are sensitive to a remarkable degree; any unusual sight or sudden shadow will cause them to disappear from ken in an instant. I have sometimes seen a large shoal of them swimming slowly backwards and forwards under the shelter of some projecting willows. I have been out of sight myself, but a very light stamp with the foot on the ground would be quite sufficient to send them down. Sometimes I fancy the organ of hearing in a chub is not at all acute, for I have been hid behind the bushes, and within six feet of the fish, a shout, and it hardly mattered how loud, made no difference whatever to them, but a stamp on the bank or waving a stick over them was another matter, they would then vanish in an instant. In all probability they can feel the vibration of a heavy tread if close to them, and their eyesight must be wonderfully good. So it behoves the angler to be very careful when negotiating a chub swim, and make the Nottingham man's motto, 'fine and far off,' one of his principal rules. Chub are wonderfully fond of basking just under the surface, especially during the summer time, and they are particularly partial to a quiet, sandy swim, where the willow boughs dip the water for this occupation. The observant angler would have no difficulty in getting near enough to these fish if he was anxious to try experiments as to their sight and hearing. Chub generally swim in shoals, so if one is captured there are probably some more in the same hole, swim, or run; but, alas, for the fisherman, sometimes the disturbance caused by playing and landing only one fish is enough to drive the rest to cover and put them off the feed for an hour or more, that is as far as that particular swim is concerned. Then, again, luck may favour the angler, and two, three or even four chub may be landed in quick succession before the swim gets disturbed and the fish driven to cover.

These fish are gross feeders, they take kindly to anything and everything in the shape of food that comes down the stream to them, it hardly matters what it is; a common garden snail may be trodden upon and then kicked into the chub stream, it will be promptly swallowed; a beetle or a big caterpillar may drop from the boughs overhead, the same chub is ready for that; a butterfly is trying to dance his way across the river, a gust of wind catches him, and he flops on the surface for just one instant, there is a boil, and that insect has gone to join the snail; a tiny mouse or a wee frog meets with a mishap and tumbles from the roots into the water, it is all the same to Mr. Chub, he has plenty of room for all these visitors; but, and here is the rub, put a hook and gut tackle into one of those things, and then see what the chub thinks of it. I know by practical experience that the angler's patience is going to get exhausted a good many times if he sticks to chub fishing for any length of time. As for baits for this fish, the real difficulty would be in determining what he would not take, rather than what he will. His bill of fare is lengthy in the extreme, and ranges from slugs and snails down to a gentle, from a gaudy salmon fly down to a tiny gnat, or from a bit of bread and cheese to a nubble of potted shrimps, with tallow cake, pith and brains, worms, wasp grub, raw beef, minnows, frogs, tail-end of crayfish, etc, etc, thrown in by way of make-weight, and sometimes it is not a little that satisfies them. I remember once baiting up a barbel swim with a lot of clipped-up worms - about the first swim I had the following day I landed a three-pound chub, and noticed a very unusual swelling under its stomach. Curious to see the reason we made a post-mortem, and found no fewer than 115 pieces of worms, big and little, in its inside - a couple of good handfuls altogether - and yet the greedy rascal was not satisfied, he must needs go and take my bait, when he had already swallowed, at the very least, 30 or 40 large lob-worms.

There is another little thing that I am anxious to bring before the novice, and that is the trick he is likely to play upon the uninitiated. Sometimes the roach and dace angler may catch a pound chub and fancy he has got hold of an extraordinary dace. These two fish, when the chub is small, have features in common, and may very readily be confounded. There are two or three differences, however, between them that will at once set the matter at rest. In the first place, closely examine the anal fin; this fin is situated underneath, between the ventral fins and the tail, and in the dace this fin, when stretched out, is concave on its edge - that is, is hollowed out - and has no sign of red colour about it. On the other hand, the corresponding fin on a chub is convex - that is, rounded off, and not hollowed out - it is also in the chub deeply tinged with red; and another test is to count the scales along the lateral line. This line can very readily be seen, broadside down the centre of the fish. In a chub the scales along this line that are marked with a dark spot, number 44, never more than 46; while on a dace the number is never less than 52. These are two unfailing tests, and should be borne in mind if any dispute arises as to the identity of these fish.

With regard to chub fishing, there is a very curious superstition on the subject that a good many of the chub fishermen of the Trent firmly believe in. I should have thought that such a prosy, everyday occurrence as chub fishing would not lend itself to the supernatural, but among the poorer class of anglers this feeling is very acute. The circumstances attending my introduction to this was as follows:- An old friend and I had made arrangements to try the chub with pith and brains in a nice eddy that could only be got at with the aid of a boat. It was a swim at the extreme end of an old stick weir, a splendid gravelly bottom, but not more than three feet deep at the outside. It was a very cold day, no wind, and the hoar frost hung heavy on every bough and tree. There had been during the late autumn a succession of heavy floods, but the cold weather set in and fined down the water nicely. We found on several former occasions that stress of heavy water would drive the chub into that little sheltered bay, and as this was the first favourable opportunity we had had for several weeks past, owing to floods, to fish it, and as Christmas was fast approaching, and the frost looked like continuing, we determined to go. At the appointed time my friend turned up, but I could see very plainly by his manner that something was up. He was growling and swearing in a frightful manner. On asking him the reason of this extraordinary demonstration I got enlightened in a bit of Nottinghamshire superstition that some of the working men chub anglers had great faith in. "Why," said he, "I met a squint-eyed woman when coming along to your place, and it is not a bit of good me going chub fishing today now, for I know, as plain as can be, that I shall have no luck." However, I only laughed it off, and we set out, but the result of the afternoon's sport was, to say the least of it, very curious. We fished side by side, out of one boat, tackle and baits exactly similar. I let him take the swim first; in fact, did everything I could to make him successful - and he was a very expert chub angler - but no; all the afternoon he only got one little chub, less than a pound in weight, while I took 13 from 2lb to 4lb each. He said he knew very well what the result would be before we started, and he might as well have stayed at home. Personally, I have no faith in these extraordinary and singular superstitions, and only looked at the affair as a bit of luck; but that man had a wonderful belief in it, and so had several more in that locality, and I have known him more than once, when going down the street fully equipped and prepared for an afternoon's chub fishing, to turn back home again and abandon his journey, or else alter his plans and go roach fishing instead, on meeting what he swore was the very unluckiest thing a chub fisherman could meet - that fateful squint-eyed woman.

CHAPTER II

WINTER CHUBBING (THE OUTFIT)

The Chub as a winter fish - The Chub rod - The centre-pin reel - Chub lines - Floats - Chub tackle - Hooks - Chub fishermen's sundries.

I hinted in the previous chapter that our friend the chub was what we may call an all-round fish, he could be taken in all sorts of weather, and under a variety of circumstances. In the first place, we will look at him as a cold-weather fish, and, like Eugene Aram, see him when:

'A mighty wind has swept the leaves,
And now the ground is bare.'

For our English chub is by no means a summer fish only, he will not only leap to the fly when the earth is scorched beneath the rays of a fierce sunshine, but he will quietly pull down your float when fishing is anything but a pleasant occupation - when ponds and lakes are fast held in the grip of the Ice King; when the hoar frost hangs in a thousand fantastic shapes from every tree; when with upturned collar and blue noses we shiver in the chill wintry blast; when every few minutes we have to suck the ice out of the rings of the rod; when fingers and hands are so benumbed that we can scarcely feel the rod and line. The stream itself must, of course, be comparatively speaking free from ice, and a clear run for the float must be obtained. Even under circumstances such as these our friend the chub will bite - aye, and bite freely - none of your Lea roach bites about him then, with just a wee tremble of the quill, but down goes your float in an instant. And fight - my word, don't they fight! If he happens to be a four-pounder he will dispute every inch of the way, and give you several anxious minutes before you creel him, especially if he has a fortress anywhere handy. I don't think the weather can be too bleak and cold for chub fishing, although I don't advise anglers to court rheumatism by fishing for him when the weather is too outrageously icy; I only mention the fact to show the vastly different conditions of weather that our leather-mouthed friend can be successfully fished for in. The chub is, in my opinion, the bottom-fisher's quarry par excellence during the cold winter months. He is then in the very pink of condition, and he seems to lose a good deal of his shyness; still you must fish for him fine and far off, approach the boughs in your boat or punt, or on the bank, in as noiseless a manner as possible, and avoid all splashing if you can. If he does then lose some of his shyness, he is still an intelligent fish, and must be treated accordingly. A four-pound chub at Christmas time, if in good condition, is a handsome fish, no matter what some carping critics may say about him, and, above all, at that time he is a sport-giving fish of a very high order. If there is one style of fishing more than another that is pre-eminently fitted for the sport now under notice, it is that style practised by the Trent adept, and known far and wide as the deadly Nottingham style.

It is a treat to see such an angler with his light, but strong, and handy rod, his easy-running wooden reel, his fine silk line, and still finer tackle, swim his float and bait away under the boughs twenty, thirty, or even forty yards, and at the dip of his float strike his fish in the twinkling of an eye. Some years ago, when I lived on the banks of the Trent, I had the distinguished privilege of fishing in the company of one of the very best fishermen that Nottingham itself could boast of. He was a queer old stick, externally rough and rugged, but he could fish a Trent chub or barbel swim. He was known to his companions as 'Old Kitty,' and he used to handle a rod that I am sadly afraid made me break the Tenth Commandment more than once in those days. It was a weapon that a fisherman could very nearly write his name with; the balance of it was perfect, it was still, fairly light, and struck beautifully direct from the point, and the play of it was grand. It bent to the pull of a heavy chub as it ought to do - down to about the centre. You could fish a whole day in comfort with that rod, and your float would go out with unerring accuracy to its swing. This rod was constructed somewhat similar to the one I so fully described in the chapter on barbel fishing, except that it was some eight or ten inches shorter, and rather lighter in material. A chub rod should be, above all things, handy and very quick in its strike and return. It need not be more than $11^1/_2$ feet in length, and should have plenty of substance in it, particularly in the lower end half. The rings on this rod should always be the first consideration; it is absolutely necessary that they should be rigidly fixed and stand stiff at right angles. The pattern, also, must be one that facilitates the easy passage of the line. I have a special liking for the ring known as the 'Bell's Life,' for the lower end of the rod, and good upright rings of a fair size on the top. It is one of the necessities of chub fishing that the line should run without catch, jerk, or hindrance, and the special rod rings just referred to are, in my opinion, the very best that have ever been invented, the chances of the line hitching or catching round them at every fresh throw is reduced to a minimum. I like plenty of backbone in my chub rods, and don't care for one of less weight than 18oz. Sometimes when chubbing in the winter, you perhaps are fishing a run under the boughs, where a lot of old roots form a cover for the fish, and your float may be some distance from you; in either of these cases the strain in trying to keep your fish away from his hover, or in giving the necessary sharp stroke to lift a long distance of line from the water and fix the hook would be something considerable. This is why I like a fairly strong rod for chubbing; but the principal thing to be considered is, this rod must strike quick and direct from the point, or you won't hook one chub out of every half-dozen bites.

The next article to be considered is a reel, and I know of no other branch of fishing where it is so necessary to have a most carefully selected reel as in this stream-fishing for chub. A first-class Nottingham man generally uses a wooden centre-pin. These reels are beautiful specimens of workmanship, and run true as a hair at the lightest touch. In inexperienced hands they are apt to be a wee bit frisky, running round like steam when they are wanted to be still, and vice versa; but when their little peculiarities are once mastered they are without doubt the very finest reels in the world for stream-fishing. Keep them properly oiled and in good condition, and they are things of joy for ever; but you must, as it were, know them, and know them well. In throwing out your bait your finger must be upon the uppermost edge of the revolving barrel, and must stop its revolutions at the right moment, or a tangle of line round your feet may ensue. See an expert use one: no paying out of line with finger and thumb, no jerking with the rod point to keep the float going, but so easily does this well-oiled reel go that your float slips down the stream like a thing of life; no stoppages, no jerking the bait off the hook, but as naturally as a piece of dried stick on the water does the stream carry it onward, the reel easily going round by itself. But see! the float stops, then shoots out of sight, and instantly the finger closes tight on the edge of the reel, and a smart strike fixes the hook. The best size for general work, and more particularly for this winter chub fishing, or, indeed, for stream fishing any time, is a three and a half inch one, and it can be made of walnut, mahogany, or ebonite, but walnut for choice. This reel should also be fitted up with a strong brass cross-back, which prevents, or, at any rate, reduces, the possibility of the back sticking and warping. Some chub fishermen like a moveable check fixed in these reels, and certainly at odd times such a contrivance is very useful, but speaking generally for the sport now under notice your reel cannot be too free and easy running. There is one thing against these reels, they are rather expensive; a good one runs to something like half a guinea, which is rather a serious item in the pocket of a working man angler; but then, on the other hand, look at the everlasting wear of them. I have had mine in constant use for something like nine or ten years, and with luck and care it looks like lasting another nine or ten. But remember, if you want your reel to be a good friend to you, you must be a good friend to it: keep it clean and as dry as you can, and in the time of need it won't fail you, but probably turn out one of the very best investments you ever made. An ordinary wooden reel for chub fishing can be got as cheap as half a crown, but they are not in the same street as the centre-pins that work on a steel point or centre, and with a spring on the front-plate. With the aid of this spring the front or barrel part of the reel can be detached from the back or spindle part in a couple of seconds and re-adjusted in its proper places with equal celerity. This is a great advantage, as sometimes a few grains of sand, or dust will work in the space between the fixed back and the revolving barrel, and so cause a grinding obstruction and prevent the free play of the reel. These can be removed, the spindle wiped clean, one single drop of oil added, and the thing is in smooth working order again, all in the space of a very few seconds; whereas the brass nut that is firmly screwed on the end of the spindle of an ordinary reel would take some considerable time screwing off if any obstruction wanted removing from the inside, or a drop of oil was necessary. I have been led to refer at some length to this subject of a reel, because it is impossible to be a successful chubber down a stream unless a proper one is used.

Years ago we old Trent men used to consider a Nottingham or Derby silk twist line the very thing for this style of stream fishing; indeed, we very often found a reel of soft-spun sewing silk, that was a suitable thickness and length, to be far and away better than the very best lines, even if the latter cost four or five times more than the former. The very best Nottingham silk twist lines, good as they were in those days, had their objections. They sometimes would in use kink or curl up; and how we used to treasure up a line that was soft and pliable and comparatively free from this kink or curl, I suppose I need not say? An old friend of mine, a well-known Nottinghamshire angler, had a very curious dodge to take the kink out of a hard twisted line (the 'snerp,' he used to call it). He ran the whole of it from his reel, so that it laid all its length on the short grass of a big meadow, then, with reel in hand, he proceeded to walk two or three times all round this meadow with the loose line trailing behind him. He maintained that a dose of this treatment effectually cured the hardest line that ever was spun. Of late years, however, the lines for chubbing down streams have been made plaited, instead of twisted; and certainly plaited lines have two great advantages over the old twisted ones: (1) they are nothing like so liable to kink in use, and (2) they are stronger with less bulk, which is a great convenience in this style of fishing. The finer your line, the easier it goes, and you can fish your swim in a much more workmanlike manner with a fine line than with a stout one. Where the stream fisherman for chub buys his line, he should stipulate for two things: first, that it must be as fine as possible; second, that it must be capable of lifting a dead weight of at least 4lb. It is rather difficult to determine the size, because, unfortunately, so many line-makers are in the market, and each have their own particular number, no two of them number the same sizes alike. The size that one maker would call a No. 2, another might call a No. 6, and so on; but, anyhow, if this will help the novice anything, I may say that the size need not be much thicker, if any, than very stout sewing thread; and if the stream he operates on is of some magnitude, he should not have less than sixty yards, nor need he have more than eighty under any circumstances.

When fishing for chub during the winter the angler is often bothered by the weather. Fogs and heavy mists are frequent, the rod gets wet, the line sticks to the rings, and everything connected with it is a general nuisance. We used to experience a great difficulty in the free and easy working of the line. This is a very important item to remember, because, to say the least of it, it is extremely unpleasant, as do what we will the float does not travel onwards with ease, as it ought to do. We have to continually jerk the rod point to keep the line going through the rings, and this gives the bait an unnatural appearance in the water. It should swim down the stream as naturally as possible, like a bit of food swept by the current into the swim. If the bait jerks up and down in the water it is calculated to cause suspicion among those keen-eyed chub. Every few minutes we have to wipe the rod dry with a pocket-handkerchief, and thus help it a bit, but the next minute it is as bad as ever again.

Nottingham Bailey, in a letter to one of the sporting papers, recommended the chub fisherman, under these circumstances, to dress the line before starting with a liberal dressing of palm oil, and certainly when tried it obviated the difficulty somewhat. An old friend, who used in days past to do a lot of chub fishing, was very much struck with that idea; he used to stretch his line down the garden path and then pour a little of this oil into a bit of flannel, and rub it well up and down the line just before he started out on a misty or heavy day; and, as he expressed it, 'it paid.' A little bit of composite candle rubbed down the line, the same as recommended for still water roach fishing, will be found very useful in floating the line, for you must bear in mind that if you can keep your line on the surface of the water, particularly in long swims, your chance of hooking the fish will be all the better.

Some chub fishermen use a heavy cork float for stream work during the winter, when one of half the size would be ample. My own idea, for even this season of the year, is that the float should be no bigger than the stream requires, of course paying regard to the depth of the water and the strength of the current. I consider a fairly stout pelican quill about eight or nine inches long, and carrying some ten or a dozen BB shot, plenty large enough for even very deep and heavy streams; while for water less deep and rapid, a swan quill seven inches long, and carrying half a dozen of the same sized shot, will be found quite big enough. I have often wondered during the last few years how it is that real good pelican quills are getting so scarce and dear; but it is so. It is very seldom indeed that a first-class one can be procured for either love or money - I mean those that are as hard as iron, as round as possible, and fairly long, stout, and thick in the barrel. Inferior kinds that are soft and somewhat flat, can be occasionally procured; a real good one is worth a trifle nowadays. Perhaps the wandering gunner with his improved arms and ammunition has had something to do with it, and before long the wild pelican will be nearly as extinct as the dodo. I, for one, am sorry that it is so, because I have a great fondness for a first-class pelican float for either chub or barbel fishing. In the chapter on barbel floats I gave a list of some half-dozen suitable for barbel fishing. I might say that the Nos. 1, 2, and 3 there described will also be capital stream floats for chub, and about all that the winter fisherman will require.

The gut bottom for this work should be about three or four feet in length, and of good quality, fairly fine in substance, but not too much so. There is no great advantage in extra fine tackle for winter chub fishing. During the summer time, perhaps, when the water is very low and bright, fine gut may be necessary, but for the time now under notice it should be capable of lifting at least 3lb dead weight. This tackle can be stained, and for winter chubbing I find no colour so good as a dark, smoky blue. There is a diversity of opinion among anglers as to the best hook for this particular purpose. Some swear by a small treble, others by a double hook, while there are those, again, who favour a single one. Even the shape is the subject of considerable discussion, round bends, sneck bends, and crystal bends having each their respective champions and adherents. I should not like to say positively that any one kind was much better than the others; they are all very good in their way, but each angler has his own fads and fancies, and I must confess that my own particular fancy is in favour of a Carlisle round bend single hook, with a fairly long shank. Treble hooks and double hooks are extremely useful when fishing with bullock's pith or scratchings; in fact, some first-class chubbers that I know use nothing else when trying the two baits just named. They say, and with some show of reason, that they stand a better chance of hooking their fish, especially at the end of a very long swim, because there are two or three points of the hook to catch hold, instead of only one, as in the case of a single hook. I must, however, caution the amateur as to the use of these small treble hooks when stream fishing for chub. Some of these hooks are made with an eye at the end of the shank, and our novice may think to himself that these eyed hooks will save a lot of trouble by being so easy to attach to his gut line; but my advice is, always when fishing down a strongish stream for chub use a hook - be it treble, double, or single - that has a taper shank, and that wants firmly whipping to the gut line. An eyed hook that swings loosely as it were at the end of the tackle very often turns out a delusion and a snare; the strength of the current, or some natural cause in its passage down the swim, causes this eyed hook to get in a very unnatural position, the bends probably pointing upwards, instead of hanging straight down, and on striking at a bite the hook is drawn out of the chub's mouth instead of into his leathery lips. I just mention these points about treble and double hooks; but, after a long experience, I fail to discover any great advantage in them over the single hooks when used in this winter chub fishing. A fair-sized single hook seems to me to have more holding power, while your bait, be it worms, or be it pith, can be put on with greater facility. I like the old-fashioned round bend hook for chub fishing, and have not much faith in some of the so-called improvements, outbarbs and sidebarbs included. Some of these improvements are in many cases nothing but theory, and when put into actual practice by an experienced angler very often turn out failures, or, at the best, only partly successful. A chub has a large mouth, and, I might add, a very tough one, and when the hook gets firmly fixed it is very seldom it cuts out; and I find by actual experience, especially in using bullock's pith, that I lose the fewest fish, after once hooking them, when my hook has been a No. 4 (Redditch scale) Carlisle round bend bright. Bear in mind, however, that I do not condemn all other hooks, double and treble, because I have used all and have done fairly well with them, but my fancy goes slightly in favour of the single round bend. The best sizes for the sport now under notice will be Nos. 6, 5, and 4, the two former for worms, and the latter for scratchings and pith. The gut tackle itself should be three or four feet of medium gut. It is not advisable, nor even safe, to use drawn gut for this purpose, or even fine undrawn. When the tackle is properly made and shotted it ought to present the following appearance:- First, we will suppose the swim you have selected to be about five to six feet deep, the current moderately strong, and the float selected a fairly stout pelican quill, or a seven-inch curved cork float capable of carrying ten BB shots. None of these shots should be at a less distance from the hook than fourteen inches, and at that sport there should be two about an inch apart; five inches above those, two more should be similarly placed, and then again seven inches above the last two; another couple should be pinched on; and nine inches above the last a pair more must be added, and so on until the whole eight, ten, or twelve, as the case may be, are fixed on, the whole of these split shots occupying from two to three feet of the gut bottom, two of them nearly together at irregular distances, varying from five to nine inches from each pair. If the float selected for the swim is a smaller one, and will only carry five or six shots, in this case put the shot on singly instead of in pairs, the distances from each other to be the same as before. I have found this plan much better than that of crowding your shot all in a heap within a foot or so of the hook; your tackle does not bag, as it were, between the float; but it seems to glide straighter and more easily down the swim; the fish have a quicker pull at the float, and your response as a natural consequence can be all the sharper, for bear in mind when chub fishing in the winter, especially with bullock's pith as bait, you cannot be too quick in striking, you must respond at the very instant the float dips, or in nine cases out of ten you will be too late, and will find that Mr. Chub has ejected the bait in the twinkling of an eye. It was this peculiarity and promptness in that fish that caused me to be so particular in my description of the outfit necessary for that work, for I would have you remember that you have not got a quiet sucking bream or cap to deal with, but a fish that is prompt in its actions, taking a bait and ejecting it with equal rapidity.

A good landing net of no less than fourteen inches in diameter, and a couple of feet deep, should also be carried; and if this net can be contrived so that it slings from your shoulder, in such a position as to be out of the way, and yet so that it can be easily brought into service for landing purposes, while one hand is still playing the fish, all the better, because this winter chubbing - or summer, indeed, for the matter of that - is best performed by what is known as roving, that is going down stream from swim to swim, trying all likely looking places en route, and stopping at none very long together, unless sport just there is very good indeed. This roving for chub during the winter is a very enjoyable amusement, and one that I used to be particularly fond of when I fished the streams and eddies of the Lower Trent and the middle reaches of the Witham; and later on I have found it just as effective down the streamy backwaters and the more rapid parts of the Bedfordshire and Huntingdon Ouse.

CHAPTER III

WINTER CHUBBING

(Hook Baits, and Ground Baits, and How to Use Them)

Bullock's pith - Brains - Scratchings - How to ground Bait - Winter haunts of Chub - A good swim and a fair bag.

My list of baits for the chub during the cold winter weather is not a very extensive one, but I think it is one that will prove ample for all practical purposes. First and foremost must be put bullock's pith and brains; second, chandler's greaves or scratchings; and third, worms. First, then, we will take bullock's pith, which is the spinal cord, and when drawn from the beast looks very dirty and disagreeable. This can be procured from the butcher's slaughter-house; if you can catch the man of poleaxe and cleaver when the bullock has been hanging two or three days, just when he is cutting the carcass into joints, a bribe of sixpence might tempt him to draw you out a good supply. When first drawn from the backbone of the beast this pith is in a long length, like a rope, and is enveloped in a thin but tough skin. To prepare it, take a pair of sharp, finely-pointed scissors, and cut this skin from end to end and carefully remove it; this outer envelope is useless; next wash the inside pith in a basin of clear, cold water till it is perfectly clean, free from blood, and all other impurities. It is now white and ready for the hook, and does not need any other preparation. Some anglers say that it should be scalded or parboiled, but I say don't be deluded into doing anything of the sort, or ten to one, you will spoil it; it is quite good enough as it is; in fact, better. After it is washed, and the water drained from it, you will find some of the pieces nearly a foot long, and almost as thick as your finger. An oval tin, or bait-box, about five inches long, by three inches wide, and an inch or so deep, will be found a capital thing to carry it in, and if this tin has a tightly fitting lid, all the better, as it then can be carried nice and handy in one of the side pockets of the angler's fishing jacket, but always be very careful to see that this tin is perfectly sweet and clean; it should be well scalded and washed before the pith is put into it, or that bait will speedily turn sour, and a musty sour bait has not much attraction for a chub. A bit about the size of a hazel-nut is about right for a bait, and this must be clipped clean from one of the lengths in the box before mentioned with the aid of sharp scissors, and carefully put on the No. 4 hook, as already recommended for this bait. Pith when fresh is nice and tough, and there is very little difficulty in getting it to stop on the hook, at least while two or three swims are taken, but do not stick the hook carelessly in one end and let it hang down below the bend, but put the hook through and through the bait a few times, and work it well up the shank. I might just mention that when you have removed the outer skin of this pith for the purpose of cleansing it, there is a finer inner skin underneath the outer one, which must be left on, and this inner skin will be found extremely useful when baiting the hook. It was for the purpose of cutting this inner envelope clean off that I recommended a sharp pair of scissors to be carried and used when baiting.

This is a capital bait for chub during the winter but in my opinion it is very little good using it unless there is a frost. I have tried it when the weather has been mild, but with only very poor results; but when the thermometer has gone down to freezing point, and several degrees below it, even as many as twelve or fifteen, then did the chub take kindly to it. As soon as the mercury got below freezing point I found the chub all the keener on it, while during the mild days of November not much could be done with that particular bait. The brains are used as ground bait, but only when pith is used upon the hook. Before using, brains should also be well cleaned and washed. Bullock's brains are by far the best, although sheep's brains can be used if none of the others are available. I have known one angler to use as many as three sets of bullock's brains in a day, but this is rather too liberal a dose. I should say a couple of sets will be ample, and he will manage very well with only one, if he cannot procure any more. I generally pay sixpence a set for bullock's brains, and if the angler has three or four lengths of pith, each about a foot long, and the thickness of his little finger, in addition to one or two sets of brains, he should stand a winter's day chub fishing and not be short of bait, that is if he uses it as judiciously as he ought for that season of the year. After the brains are washed and cleaned they must be boiled; it will be found the best plan to tie them up in a white, clean rag, and put them in a saucepan with plenty of water, and then boiled for twenty minutes after the water reaches the boiling stage. As soon as they are cold they are quite ready for use, and do not require mixing with anything else, or any other preparation whatever. Some anglers carry them down to the riverside in a tin or a small bait can, but I prefer to tie them up in a clean, white rag. Some also chop them up very small before they start; others chew them up and eject them from their mouths in small quantities while fishing. I generally put a piece about twice the size of the hook bait into the palm of my left hand, and with pocket-knife or scissors cut it up as small as I possibly can. I throw it on the water, taking care that it goes down the stream as fine as snowflakes, and directly in the track of the float, repeating this from time to time as occasion requires; and, above all, taking care that in case there is a good stream it is thrown in high enough up stream, or well above where I stand, so that it is not carried out of reach, or swept away by the current far past the place where I want the hook bait to travel in. I have just spoken of brains as ground bait, and it is a general thing for most chub fishermen to call them by that term; but when we come to look fairly at the matter it can hardly be so dubbed. Chub generally feed on the surface, or in midwater, and sometimes at the bottom. These particles of brains are really intended as an attraction to lure the fish outside their fortresses of old roots, boughs, or hollow banks, and set them on the work in the swim itself. I have frequently seen chub rise and take a morsel of this bait close to the surface of the water. Ground bait, as we understand it for roach, bream, or barbel, is made so that it sinks quickly to the bottom of the swim and stays there, or at least as much as can be expected, according to depth and strength of current. Chub, as a general rule, care not ground-baited for in the same manner; it is simply a very little bit of something attractive whirling about in the streams and eddies, and it does not matter whether this reaches the bottom or not, so long as the chub have a chance of seeing it, and it is successful in luring them outside their strongholds. A chub will rise to meet the bait; in the case of barbel you must keep your bait along the bottom, or he cannot, or will not, get it as a general thing. Mr. Chub is at home anywhere, surface, midwater, or bottom, it is all the same to him. If the bait does not go down to him he will rise to the bait, and this is the reason I recommend only small portions, and these clipped up as fine as possible, to throw in when fishing down a stream during the winter for chub. But to proceed. Greaves or scratchings are the refuse of the tallow chandler's melting pot when compressed into hard and solid blocks. It is extremely difficult nowadays to get good English tallow cake. The old-fashioned tallow candle factory seems to be gradually going out of date; we may find an odd one or two in some out-of-the-way corners of England, but the composite candle seems to be improving the old ones off the face of the earth, and alas for the sport of the barbel and chub fishermen that it should be so. You can easily procure foreign tallow cake, black and disagreeable, but it is hardly fit for ground bait. All the goodness is squeezed out of it before it is landed in old England. It lacks entirely when boiled that luscious, greasy look, those white and tempting tit-bits so beloved by the barbel and chub fishermen, and that appetising smell. When you do happen to be so lucky as to find a block of first-class English tallow cake, treasure it up most carefully, for it will keep good for many months while kept in a hard and solid lump. To prepare it for bait you must knock from the block a lump a bit bigger than your fist; this will be plenty for winter fishing, and with a hammer pound it up small, put it in a saucepan, add sufficient water to well cover it, and boil it over the fire from twenty minutes to half an hour, until well cooked. Care should be taken that the saucepan is large enough, and don't stint water, as scratchings when boiled swell out to double, and even treble, the bulk that they were when dry and hard. When cooked enough, which will easily be seen by the mass looking and feeling soft, the water should be drained from them, and as soon as cool they are ready for use. I must here give one word of advice, don't cook too much at once, because after scratchings are boiled they speedily turn sour. I would not advise them to be kept longer than two days at the outside. At one time I simply used to pour boiling water over them, cover them down close in a jar or gallipot, and stand them on one side to cool, but I found out by actual practice that it was a great deal better when boiled. The white pieces are used for the hook, and those nice, greasy-looking, tempting, pipey bits should be chosen, and being tougher and more lasting on the hook than pith, it does not present so much difficulty in baiting; but be careful not to bury the hook point right in the middle of the bait, or you cannot strike your fish. Bring the point out somewhere, and if you think the hook point looks too conspicuous put a tiny bit more on it. The same size hook as recommended for pith will do well for scratchings, and the angler can use a double hook in this case if he likes, as a double hook is extremely killing with this bait; but for my own part I prefer the single one. The commoner, dark-coloured, and smaller bits of tallow cake can be used as ground bait, but remember what I said in the case of bullock's brains, and treat this as near as you can like that. Clip it up as small as ever you possibly can, and when chub fishing in the winter use it as sparingly as possible, a few very small pieces thrown in as you go along being quite sufficient. This bait is the best during the early part of the winter, say from the beginning of October to the latter end of November, and if the weather is open right through the winter, provided the water is low and bright, as this is a bait that is more deadly in a low, clear water than in any other. I have known chub to be taken during the winter by the aid of strange morsels, such as a scrap of boiled tripe, a little bit of fat beef, or even a shred of lean beef or ham; but for my own part, if I can anyhow procure good tallow cake or bullock's pith I most certainly prefer it. If the water is coloured by rain, or fining down after a flood, perhaps a worm then will be the best winter bait, and two or three cockspurs, or the tail-end half of a well-scoured maiden lob on a No. 6 hook may be successful in luring an odd chub or two, but the angler had better stay at home than fish for chub when melting snow and ice are tearing down the river in high flood. It is very little good trying either pith, tallow cake, or any other bait of a similar character in a flooded, coloured water; these are essentially fine-water baits, and must be treated and used as such. An old Nottinghamshire chub fisherman, one of the old school of anglers, told me some little time ago that when he used to fish forty years ago, chub fishing was something like sport. "Lor' bless yer," said he, "them chub weren't half so particular in those days as they are now; I could dig a few worms out of the garden, rough and ready, they did not want scouring in moss nor anything else, and go down to the river and catch half a dozen almost any time in an hour or two; and it did not matter where I tried so long as there was a bit of a stream and a clear bottom, for chub were all over the place. As for the depth of winter, why, a handful of boiled tallow cake would fill a basket with 'em during a short afternoon's fishing." This is the testimony of one of the oldest and best anglers the Trentside can boast of; but it is vastly different nowadays, and we sometimes wonder why the chub have altered so in their tastes; everything has to be specially prepared. No 'rough and ready' bait, as noted above will do for them. Perhaps the solution of the problem must be looked for in the march of civilisation. Even mankind some two or three centuries ago were very primitive in their habits, and used by way of food, articles that even the very poorest nowadays would turn from in disgust, so with the chub, gradually they have been educated up to their present standard of refined taste. Now you have to know, as it were, the haunts and habits of the fish, and exercise the greatest care and caution to have anything like success with them. Some odd times, if the fates are in your favour, you may have a slice of rattling luck, and land a dozen good fish, while at others you may toil all day and catch nothing. Success depends in a great measure on knowing the most likely haunts of the fish. An inexperienced eye might fish a swim that looked the very beau ideal of a chub swim without a single bite all down its course. There might be a variety of reasons why no chub were in it, in spite of its very promising look, while water that contained chub might be passed over as looking unsuitable for the sport. If the angler does not know the water it is a good plan to leave hardly any of it untried, two or three swims with his bait being quite sufficient for one place if he gets no response, as a chub is a fish that in the winter, if he means to take, will take either the first or second swim down. If you don't get a bite after the third or fourth swim down, shift a little lower down stream, and keep repeating this operation till you do find the fish at home, and be sure to remember what I said a little while ago, cut up your ground bait as fine as ever you can, use it as sparingly as possible, and let your hook bait travel the first swim down close on the heels of the ground bait; that is, have your hook bait all ready, and directly the morsels of ground bait start on their journey throw in your tackle, and let it go in close pursuit. By following this dodge anglers have succeeded in luring some very good chub to their destruction.

Personally, I don't like a very deep swim for chub. From four to six feet is the best, and where a steady stream flows over a gravelly, or better still a sandy, bottom. A sure find is under a row of willows, where the roots afford a cover for the fish, and the overhanging boughs dip the water. Yet even a place like this I have known tenantless of chub, where the bottom has been muddy and the stream too sluggish, so, perhaps, it will be as well if I just qualify my statement, and say it is a sure find provided the bottom and the stream are right. Perhaps you may have noticed, in streams like the Trent, the water flowing along smoothly for a few yards, then, as it were, stopping to curl round, and going on again for a few yards, then another curl of the water, and so on. These sort of places are the haunts and homes of chub, and ought not to be missed on any account. I have found them during the winter in less than three feet of water, and in a shallow, quiet corner just on the edge of a stream. It does not matter if the water is no great depth in these eddies and curls, close under the bank, where a good stream rattles on outside, they should not be lost sight of on any pretence. Drop the bait on the edge between stream and curl, and let it go down till it is swept well into the eddy, and in all probability a nice fish would be the result. In a stream like the Trent, that is subject to heavy floods, the banks often get undermined, and holes are swept out by the tearing flood water, and along these places, to prevent the river encroaching on the land too much, a lot of faggots, or rough bundles of thorns and branches are firmly staked in the water during low water time and filled up between the said faggots and the banks with stones, gravel, earth, or any other old rubbish they have handy. The water alongside these old sticks, etc., ought to be well tried, for very often large chub lie lurking under their shadow. A bit of bush that dips the water, no matter how unpretending it looks, often has a couple of good chub lurking in its immediate vicinity. The tail-end of an old stick weir that divides the stream, as it were, into two parts, and causes an eddy between these two streams, ought to be well tried, even if the water is shallow, as I have taken some of my best chub during the winter from places such as these; in fact, it will pay the winter chub fisherman to try all sorts of streamy places, curly corners just away from the main current, under boughs and bushes, alongside old piles and woodwork, by the side of stick weirs and bush-mended banks, the places to avoid being deep, sluggish water with a muddy bottom, as chub do not often frequent places like that. I have in my mind's eye now a swim down the Lower Trent that I once, some years ago, took a full dozen good chub from during a Christmas Bank Holiday afternoon. It was a cold, frosty day, but the way those fish pulled down the float was a caution, and I must have lost as many fish as I took by being unable to keep them clear of the old roots and submerged boughs. The swim was only some two or three hundred yards long, but every yard was fishy. All along the bank, and projecting some considerable distance into the stream, was a row of willows that afforded capital shelter for the chub; in fact, I found out by broken tackle and lost fish that this shelter was rather too much in evidence. The bottom of the river was clean sand, with a nice gentle stream, and the depth close to the willows did not average above four feet. Pith and brains was the bait I used, and I fished every yard carefully, tying the boat to the boughs with a stout cord at every fresh place or swim I wished to try, taking particular care that the boat was never less than ten or a dozen yards from unfished water. My bag at night contained fourteen chub, largest $3^3/_4$lb, smallest $1^1/_2$lb. No part of that water was more than five feet deep, and some of it was under three feet; and the weather, as I have already hinted, was very cold and frosty. So the novice will see that even in winter a great depth of water is not an actual necessity; indeed, I remember once getting a brace of real good chub out of a smart run under a thorn bush, where the water was so clear and shallow that my gut bottom only contained one single strand of gut; and, on the other hand, I have got them when the bait has been twelve feet from the float. It is impossible to lay down a hard and fast line in this matter; all sorts of likely-looking swims, at all sorts of depths, must be tried if the angler wishes to be a successful winter chubber.

During very cold weather it is necessary that the fisherman should wear a good pair of waterproof shoes and leggings, a good warm overcoat, and as gloves are very awkward in baiting a hook or taking the fish off the tackle, I recommend a pair of woollen mittens with a hole for the thumb, and reaching up to the knuckles, as these keep the ends of the fingers free, and yet they are nice and warm for the wrists and the back of the hands.

CHAPTER IV

SUMMER CHUBBING (WITH THE FLOAT)

Chubbing in the summer - The Outfit - Baits - Wasp grubs; how to take, and how to prepare - Fishing a Chub stream - Cheese, and cheese paste - Minnow fishing - A curious Chub adventure.

In this chapter I propose to look at the chub from a far different standpoint to what I did in the two preceding ones. Then I discussed him as a winter fish, when the banks and the weather were anything but comfortable, and fishing decidedly not of the butterfly order. Now we will look at him from pleasant surroundings, when the sun has warmed up the earth and the water, when tree and bush are putting on their gayest attire, when thousands of insects are constantly on the wing, and the birds are singing out their hearts in thankful strains. The subject of summer chub fishing opens out a wide field; because as I remarked in the opening chapter this fish can be captured in a greater variety of ways and by a greater variety of baits during the summer and early autumn, than any other fish I am acquainted with. Each different stream and river, however, that I have followed this sport in, seems to have some special characteristic of its own; the style that is so deadly down the streams of the Trent, the Thames, and kindred rivers, cannot well be practised on the backwaters and bush grown weedy streams of the Ouse; the wide open shallows of the Trent want negotiating in a different manner to the quiet chubby corners of the Bedfordshire river. But I must hasten to say that the novice may console himself with the fact, that no matter what river he haunts, the chub is a chub in all of them; and is captured in much the same way and by the same baits in most of them; although the method of presenting those baits to the notice of Mr. Chub materially differs on various waters. It was that, and that alone, I had in my mind's eye just now, when I hinted that the style so deadly down one stream, could not well be followed in another. The outfit for summer chubbing, that is, for fishing with the float, can be similar to the one I described in Chap. 2; the rod and reel exactly the same, the line, however, can be a trifle finer; say a very stout roach line, for size; this line should be at least sixty yards long, and care should be taken that it is good in quality, and capable of lifting at least three pounds at a dead pull; a slight dressing of King's Ceroleum will be an advantage to the line in this stream fishing for chub, for reasons that I have explained elsewhere. It is absolutely necessary that the reel should run with the utmost freedom, and that the tackle itself should be as fine as possible consistent with strength; a tackle three or four feet long will be ample, and this should be stained and shotted in exactly the same manner as described for winter chubbing. If the gut line will, like the silk line, stand a dead pull of three pounds, it will with care kill chub of large size. Hooks for summer chubbing are the same as for winter, viz., 4, 5, 6, and 7, round bend, bright, Carlisle pattern. Floats can be summed up in a word or two. The Nos. 1, 2, and 3 described in the chapter on barbel floats being sufficient for almost any emergency. If the stream is only moderate in flow, and not very deep, the No. 1 will do, particularly during low and clear water; if rather deeper and heavier the No. 2 can be employed, while for deep holes and strong curls try the No. 3 cork float. These if shotted correctly will fish any chub swim; in fact, to put it as briefly as I possibly can, the instructions laid down in the two preceding chapters on how to fish a stream during the winter will answer admirably for the summer, the manipulation of the rod, reel, line, floats, and tackle being identical in both cases; it is only the bait that differs. As soon as the season opens the cad-bait is the most likely lure; two or three of them on a No. 6 or 7 hook, swum down any and every curl, eddy, and swim (it hardly matters how shallow the water is, provided there is a stream handy and the bottom clean) will be found a bait that the chub, at that season of the year, can hardly resist. Ground bait with a handful or two of coarse gentles, or a ball or two of the bread and bran described in roach fishing; and always remember in chub fishing that more sport can be obtained by roving about. A few swims here, and a few swims there, casting in the smallest amount of ground bait possible as you go along down stream. I won't trouble to repeat what I said about where to look for chub, as the remarks already penned in the preceding chapter will tell the novice all he wants to know on the subject. They haunt much the same places during the summer as they do in the winter; of course, while they are on the shallows after spawning being excepted. Gentles are another good bait during the early summer, a good mouthful, say six or seven well scoured yellow ones on a No. 6 or 7 hook, swum down their haunts will very often fetch them. I remember, twenty years ago, when I used to fish the river Witham - in some parts of its course - between Long Bennington and Norton Disney, what bags of chub I got during the early summer with gentles; the Trent also yielded well to that bait. If a flush of water comes down the river, and a trifle of colour with it, then two or three lively cockspurs, dropped into all sorts of curly corners, eddies at a dyke end, the back of a bush, under an overhanging bank, or any similar position, even if no more than a yard from the side, would often result in unexpected sport. All sorts of strange baits can be tried at a pinch, say a large peeled shrimp, a small black slug, that has been trodden upon, so that his white insides protrude; a lump of white, red, or yellow paste, and in some waters the tail of a crayfish is the very finest bait that can be swum down a chub stream. As soon as the summer gets a little further advanced, about the time say that the plums are getting ripe, then the wasp grub is by far the best bait to try; I should suppose everybody knows a wasps nest when he sees one, and how to take it. I might, however, just tell the novice that it is as well to be very careful during the process of storming the wasp's fortress; an accurate survey of the exact locality should be made from a safe distance during daylight, and carefully marked; a little after sunset is the time for storming. Armed with a spade, a bag, and a squib, which latter article I may say in passing is made out of a couple or three ounces of common fine black gun-powder, damped with water, and rolled into a long, oval-shaped ball, Devil's heads we used to call them in boyhood's days, something like three inches long and an inch thick, a little dry powder being just dabbed on one end; our angler proceeds with muffled foot-steps, and as much caution as a professional housebreaker, carefully clears out the entrance hall. The wasps have now retired to rest, and only a late straggler or two are seen about the door of the castle; the squib is set on fire at the end where the dry powder is, and instantly thrust into the hole as far as it will go; then pushed gently down with a stick, a bit of grass sod should be promptly put over the hole and stamped tight in with a boot heel. An interval for refreshment, say five or ten minutes pull at the pipe, is the next item on the programme, by which time if the powder squib worked all right and spluttered itself out, the wasps have become hypnotised, and the cakes of grubs can be dug out. Lift each one carefully out, brush with a small bunch of grass all loose wasps off, pop them in the bag, and vanish as quickly as may be. This concludes the performance for the time being. Some wasps' nests contain only two cakes, one above the other; others contain as many as five, some of them being as far about as a dinner plate, or even more, and containing a very large quantity of grubs. The cakes will be found to contain grubs in various stages of development; some small and maggot-like in appearance; others larger, dull yellow in colour, and more juicy, with no sign of legs or wings about them. Others, again, are white, showing very plainly the eyes, wings and legs. Some, again, are rapidly changing into wasps; so much so, that the black stripes on the body can be distinctly seen. The large ones, that show no signs of what they will be, are the best for the hook - the grubs pure and simple, those that have one end uncovered, and which work about in a peculiar manner; these grubs are still being fed. As soon as they are fed up fully, the parent wasps seal them down, each one in his own particular cell, for a single glance will tell the novice that the cakes contain a quantity of small cells, each one having its own occupant. As I have just said, those that are uncovered and still feeding are by far the best for the hook; all the rest can be used as groundbait. I prefer to use these grubs just as they are without any previous preparation. I fancy the sticky glutinous fluid, that smells and tastes a good deal like honey, and which is found only on the feeding grubs, to be the great attraction with this bait. One thing, however, is against keeping the cakes of grubs in their original state, and that is, every few hours fresh wasps hatch out, crawl out of their cells, and make things decidedly unpleasant; but personally I would much rather suffer these little unpleasantnesses than bake or boil them. Some of my old friends recommended the cakes to be put into a hot oven for five minutes and baked; others said they (that is, the good grubs) should be carefully picked out of the cakes and put in a jar; then this jar should be set inside a saucepan of water and boiled over the fire for ten minutes, great care being taken that not one drop of water goes inside the jar among the grubs. These operations most certainly do toughen them, so that they stop on the hook better. Another old friend recommended the cakes to be broken up in three or four pieces and steamed, the same as potatoes are steamed above a large saucepan of boiling water; the best of the grubs to be then picked out and dropped into a mixture of sweetened water and treacle that is slightly flavoured with rum. He maintained that grubs treated in this manner will keep good for three or four weeks, and preserve their aroma and whiteness. Well perhaps they may, but I know by a practical experience of the subject, that grubs from a freshly-procured nest, alive and kicking, are the most attractive. My plan is to take the cakes down to the river in a bag, pick out all the good grubs from one of them, and put them in a tin; these being reserved for the hook. As soon as I got to a suitable stream or swim, a little of the cake, half-grown wasps and all, is crumbled up into small pieces and thrown on the water; these do not sink. I then keep an eye on the floating morsels. Perhaps before they have travelled ten yards down stream there is a boil in the water under them, then another. This generally means that chub are in the swim, and are rising to inspect the strange fare floating over them. Now, quick! on with three or four grubs; judge the distance and depth, but three or four feet from float to hook will be plenty for even a five or six feet swim. Drop the bait on the water carefully, for remember it is very tender, and likely to be jerked off very easily, and let it go without check or hindrance down the stream in the track of the floating fragments; and don't be frightened at a strong and rattling current, for very often in these streams heavy fish lie. Search the water by degrees with this bait, or, indeed, any other when fishing for chub in a similar manner. Try ten yards the first few swims, then fifteen the next, then twenty; and so on until you cover as much as forty yards at a single swim, if the character of the place makes it anyhow possible for such a long swim; fine and far off must be the chub fisherman's motto. Fishing the swim by degrees, as just noted, does not disturb so much water at once. It is just possible that the bait may travel the whole distance of a very long swim without a response, until the extreme end is reached, when a good one is firmly hooked. In playing it back to the rod point through water practically unfished, it is only natural to suppose that the commotion made may alarm any others that are in the intervening water. For this bait I prefer a good-sized hook, say a No. 4, and a good mouthful of grubs put on at once, even as many as half-a-dozen; if a small hook is used, and only one grub, small dace and bleak will continually annoy you, robbing the hook time after time. When this bait is in its prime, the majority of the chub have left the sandy shallows, and taken up their quarters in their usual autumn haunts under overhanging banks, roots, boughs, bushes and willows; in fact, all such places as indicated in a previous chapter, and should be searched for in any and every swim that has any pretence at all to a curly, eddying stream with a sandy or gravelly bottom. August and September are the best months for the grub, and I might add that all sorts of fish, as well as chub, are wonderfully fond of that bait - trout, dace, roach, bream, tench, carp, and even eels being particularly susceptible to its charms.

Another real good chub bait for use during the autumn is cheese and cheese-paste, and the more this cheese smells, the better those fish like it. The angler should procure two or three pounds of old stock cheese from the provision dealers, and if it has been thrown into a corner of a cellar until the smell of it can very nearly be heard, and your next-door neighbour wonders if the drain has gone wrong, why! that is exactly the article; it can, I dare say, be purchased for twopence a pound or perhaps less. This is used in exactly the same way as wasp-grubs, a bit half an inch square (or round, the shape does not matter) being put on a No. 4 hook, and swum down the stream or under the boughs. For groundbait, crumble a little bit of the same cheese up into small fragments, and cast in directly in the track of the float; use this groundbait very sparingly, and rove about to every likely, or even unlikely, swim. Cheese-paste is made by mixing half cheese and half stiff bread-paste together, and used in the same manner. Groundbait can be made out of a ball or two of bread and bran, into which a small lump of the cheese has been well incorporated. This is useful as a bait if the angler cannot procure a good supply of cheese, and wants to spin what little bit he has out to the best advantage. And don't forget the hint already given: crumble the groundbait into the smallest fragments, use as little as possible, and let the hook bait travel down the swim close on the heels, and in hot pursuit, of the atoms of groundbait directly they are thrown in. To put this stream fishing for chub during the summer and autumn into as comprehensive a shape as possible, so that the float-fisher or the novice can make no mistake, I might say that during June and July cadbaits and a bunch of maggots will be found the best; during August and September, wasp-grubs and cheese; during September and October, cheese and scratchings; while to come to the late autumn and winter that is from October round to March, scratchings and pith and brains can generally be relied on. These are the principal baits for chub, used on float tackle, and the water should be in all cases clear, or, at least, very nearly so. For a clouded or thick water anytime, nothing will beat worms. Of course, any other baits I recommend are only what we may call chance lures, to be employed in case the regular stock baits fail; but, mind you, paste and other fancy items are none the less useful on a pinch for all that.

Another bait that is used on float tackle during the summer for chub is a live minnow. These are more successful on the sandy slacks, where the water is not very deep nor the current very strong. The tackle generally used for this lure is about a couple of feet of good gut, shotted to carry the No. 3 cork float, and mounted with a small treble on the end of the gut, and a little sliding lip hook an inch or so above it. One hook of the treble is inserted under the root of the minnow's back fin, and the lip hook firmly through the top lip. This bait should be swum a few inches above the bottom of the river, and thrown into all sorts of likely nooks and corners. As soon as the float goes under with a bite when using minnow, wait a second or two and then strike with a gentle twitch. I forgot to say a little while ago, when describing stream fishing with wasp-grubs and any similar lure for chub, that the strike should be as quick as possible; the very instant the float dips respond with a smart but not heavy stroke up stream; the delay of a second may be fatal to your chance of hooking this fish. I will conclude this chapter by giving a curious adventure a friend and I had when fishing a very awkward swim for chub. This swim was alongside a row of willows that grew on an overhanging bank. Successive floods had undermined those banks, exposing a good many of the roots, which twisted under water in all sorts of fantastic shapes; careful trials on several occasions showed the depth to be six feet on the average close to the old roots. In those days the place was a veritable chub paradise; shoals of those fish were all down its course; but if ever we were fairly and squarely licked, those chub did it. It was not because we could not hook them, or, indeed, land some of them; fish of a pound or so we could haul up to the boat without much ceremony. But the giants of the place, the four, five and six-pounders, simply refused to be hauled out, even when fairly hooked.

Time after time we swam the wasp-grubs and the cheese from the bow of the boat right into their haunts, and sometimes hooked heavy fish; the next instant there would be a heavy plunge, a sudden rush, and the tackle was fixed immoveable as a rock under the bank, and no amount of coaxing could, or ever did, shift it. We tried all sorts of dodges, but no! a broken tackle was generally the result. We found out after a few failures, by feeling carefully with a boat-hook that the bank was undermined at least a yard beyond the old roots, and the first rush of the fish was towards this impregnable stronghold; it did not matter if we used the very strongest gut; it was all the same as far as the large ones were concerned. At length my old friend thought that if we could get the rod point by any means below the old roots, and play the fish towards the bottom of the river, instead of towards the surface, we might stand a chance of nailing an odd one occasionally. Accordingly one day we put it into practice. First mooring the boat further away from the boughs than usual, after several trials and twice being broken, my friend's efforts were crowned with success. As soon as he got a bite he struck, and then thrust the rod point overboard, feeling for the bottom of the river, as it were, and winding hard on the reel. Inch by inch, fighting desperately all the way, came that chub, and after five minutes' tussle it was ours. Five pounds nine ounces it weighed, and now stares down with glassy eyes from its case on the walls of my old chum's front room. This adventure may give some puzzled chub fisherman a hint, and if he knows of a similar place, where the roots are nearly at, or only just under the surface, with a considerable depth of clear water below them, a downward playing of the fish; instead of the rod point being up in the air, put it down towards the bottom of the river, may be the means of getting a specimen. A strong old barbel rod that the angler does not care about should be used in this dodge. This is, however, a very exceptional case. I can only remember that one swim, and even there it was heartbreaking work, for every big chub we landed cost us at least three or four broken tackle, so we had to confess at last that the game was hardly worth the candle; but I give the circumstance for what it is worth.

CHAPTER V

SUMMER CHUBBING (ON THE SURFACE)

(Natural and Artificial Flies and Insects)

A typical 'dibbling' stream - A water jungle - O! those cunning Chub - The 'dibbling' outfit - How to dibble - On hooking and playing a Chub under difficulties - The fly fishing outfit - Chafer and frog fishing - Artificial flies and insects.

There appears to me to be at least two or three different ways of fishing for chub on the surface of the water, one of the most important being by means of a live insect poked carefully over their haunts by the help of a long stiff rod, and from the shadow of trees and bushes. Another plan is by wielding a fly rod from the open with artificial flies as bait. Still another method is by using a double-handed fly rod, casting all sorts of heavy insects, such as beetles and cockchafers, both natural and artificial. In order to make my remarks as plain as possible, I will first of all treat of 'dibbling,' or, as it is called in some places, 'daping.' This is a branch of fishing that is best practised on narrow rivers and streams that have a succession of deep holes and shallows all down their course, where all sorts of water vegetation luxuriate in great abundance, and where the banks are lined with trees, bushes, and huge beds of tall reeds. During my wanderings after sport I have seen several streams and rivers where this style can be successfully adopted in; in fact, it would be very difficult indeed to fish them by any other method. In Wales I saw a stream or two of that character; likewise in the Midlands, and also in Lincolnshire and the Eastern counties. One of the best, or rather, I might say, a succession of the best streams that ever I had a chance of fishing in, are found in the Bedfordshire and Huntingdonshire districts of the Ouse. These streams are peculiarly adapted for the sport of 'dibbling'; and as they are types of dozens more that are to be found in various other districts, I will describe them and the modus operandi. It was not in the main river itself that I found the chub the most plentiful, but in those backwaters and streams that left the river here and there; and after flowing and winding about across the meadows for a mile or two found their way into the river again, generally below some weir, thus getting the benefit of a drop and rather more stream than is found in the main river. In these stretches of water I found the big chub cunning and crafty to a remarkable degree. Even in the clear runs it was very little good trying for them by the ordinary Nottingham style, floating down the stream with fine tackle, when the water was clear, and at ordinary summer level. During September, when the wasp-grub was plentiful, a nice bag or two could be made by those means; but it was heartbreaking work, not one fish out of every half dozen would go a pound; small fish would continually rob the hook or insist on being hauled ashore. Besides the haunts of those fish would be in a very many places perfect jungles of flags, reeds, weeds, roots, and branches, and it is only here and there that a clear run of three or four yards could be obtained.

In these clear runs, if a worm, or a lump of cheese, or a small frog, or a black slug, or any other bait could be cunningly thrown at the end of a long line, occasional success might attend the efforts. The places were few and far between where the deadly Nottingham float fishing style could be practised with any hope of success. This being so, I speedily found that four out of every six swims would have to be operated on by 'dibbling,' if I meant to capture chub of any size. In the fine stretches of the Ouse that flow from St. Neots right away down to St. Ives, comprising many miles of water, there are many places where chub are to be found, more or less in large numbers. I have seen huge shoals of them swimming slowly round and round in the pools below the sluice gates, and in the streams that flow below the paper mill at St. Neots, under the willows and bushes at Wray House Island, in the over-fall pools at Offord and Brampton; while the backwaters and streams that skirt the Hinchingbrooke estate and intersect the parishes of Godmanchester and the Hemmingfords literally swam with them. One of the best streams in the locality is a small one, known locally as 'Lee's Brook.' It is only about one and a half miles long, and leaves the river at a place called Brampton Wale, flowing over an old stone and wooden weir, and after a short but winding course rejoins the river again some distance lower down. I select this stream because it is a good type of a 'dibbling' water, and my remarks are likely to be useful to any novice who happens to be fixed near a similar one, and also I select it because the topography and general surroundings are eminently suited for the growth and well-being of its finny inhabitants. In the summer and autumn the water is well nigh hidden in places by a dense growth of flags and water weeds, and when a good stream is running, the tall rushes in the water shake and tremble, producing a very curious effect. Swarms of butterflies, principally the red admiral, the peacock, and the clouded yellow during their season haunt the banks. Large sedge flies by hundreds crawl up the stems of the flags; grasshoppers jump about in all directions, and the pretty long-horned musk beetles are found on the willows along the brink. In fact there appears to me to be an abundance of natural fish food close at hand; and when we add the fact that the stream from one end to the other is a succession of rapid shallows and deep holes, it is not to be wondered at if the chub are plentiful and remarkably cunning and crafty. Very nearly the only way to circumvent their cunning was to use cunning yourself, and like the illustrious Caleb Plummer, 'get as near to nature' as possible'; in fact, use nature itself. You must approach them with the greatest caution, take advantage of every bit of cover, crawl up to them on all fours, if need be, and peer through the flags or bushes; and if you have conducted your operations as silently and craftily as possible, you will probably see a shoal of a dozen or more, ranging in weight from one pound up to five or six pounds each, swimming slowly round and round in a circumscribed area within two or three inches of the surface of the water. In the majority of cases, where this style can be practised, it is not a difficult matter to hide yourself, as these shoals usually select a small clear shallow, well under the shadow of the boughs. I have hinted that you have probably seen such a shoal, have come prepared for action, and in your waistcoat pocket reposes a matchbox, or some other suitable receptacle, containing a few natural insects picked up from the ground or on the bushes. Now take a beetle, or a moth, or a bee, and gently throw it on the water, as if it had dropped from the boughs overhead. In an instant an old chub wheels round; you can fairly hear the smack as his white lips open and close, and the insect has gone. Repeat this two or three times, and then you triumphantly say to yourself, 'I'll have a hook fixed in the next one, my boys.' Perhaps you select a fine fat bumble bee, and after being guided by circumstances as to how your rod and line can best be projected over the water, drop him carefully down, but with a hook tenderly inserted in him this time. That bee treads the water prettily like a thing of life, or rather like a strong winged insect trying to escape, and your heart is in your mouth as one of the biggest of the shoal rises for him with open jaws. He comes with a rush to within an inch of that bait, and then suddenly stops, and backs off a foot or so. Three or four of his comrades now join him, and they swim up and inspect that bee from every standpoint, as much as to say: 'Why, that must be a bee; but is it a safe investment, or only a modern invention?' You then throw on the water a similar bee to the hooked one, and there is no hesitation now - it is gulped down at once. I have tried all sorts of things for an hour or more over one shoal, and know of nothing more aggravating than those crafty old chub, who promptly take in everything thrown to them, except that particular thing which happens just then to have a hook in it. Of course, they make a mistake some odd times, and a good plan I have found was when the chub swam up and refused it, to carefully lift the bait from the water and drop it gently behind them. Many a good one have I taken by this simple expedient. You can hardly use a wrong bait for this style of fishing, as Mr. Chub will at times take almost anything, from a common garden snail to a bluebottle fly; all kinds of moths, bees, and butterflies, slugs, snails, and beetles; in fact, any mortal thing that turns up on the banks or hedgerows of that description he might take, if you happened to catch him in a taking humour, which, alas, does not appear to be very often, that is as far as a bait with a hook in it is concerned. I am now alluding, bear in mind, to summer fishing on the surface, when the water is very low and gin-bright. It is a far easier matter to make a bag when the water is slightly clouded, and the conditions of weather and stream favourable for the sport. The common five-spot burnet moth is a rare killer, while a ghost moth dibbled just before the dusk of evening has proved fatal to many a big chub. A large natural stone fly is a good bait, and a very lifelike imitation with gauze wings was patented and made by Messrs. Allcock, of Redditch, some time ago. This was about one of the most natural looking artificial insects I ever saw or used, and some of the best chub taken in this locality during the past few seasons were taken by its agency; they, however, cost eightpence or ninepence apiece, which is rather against their universal use in these weed-grown dibbling waters, as breakages, owing to natural obstructions in the streams, are frequent. The best rod for this work is a strong East India cane bream rod about fourteen feet long, and made in four lengths; it should be fairly stiff, and be fitted with good ferruled joints; the rings on this rod must be upright, and no larger than possible. Any sort of a common wooden reel will do, so long as it is strong and fairly free as to its running. The line itself may be twenty yards of strong barbel line, and the tackle is simply a stout gut hook, one single length of gut a foot long, mounted with a No. 5 or 6 round-bend or sneck-bend hook, according to fancy (the latter for choice). There is no advantage in using very fine tackle for this style of fishing, as the gut is seldom or never deep in the water, the object of the angler being to play the insect on the surface; besides, if the chub does gulp down the bait, strong tackle is necessary to hold him, and stop his wild rushes into the nearest weed-bed or fortress of old roots and boughs.

The outfit of a 'dibbler' is as simple as possible, with the exception of the rod and the landing-net; a couple of shillings will represent the total outlay. Of course, no float is used under any circumstances. A couple of large split shots are pinched on the silk line close to where it is joined to the gut, or perhaps a very small bullet, no larger than a green pea, with a hole drilled through the centre will be better than shot. Thread the line through the small hole in this bullet and tie the end firmly into the loop of the gut hook. In baiting with a live insect, care should be taken when inserting the hook that as little damage to it as possible is done. If the bait is a beetle or a cockchafer, put the point of the hook in the parting between the two shields or wing covers, and just stick it sideways, so that a little bit of the edge of one of those wing covers hangs on the bend of the hook. A small frog is another capital bait to dibble with, the best for the purpose being those that are only about half-an-inch in length, exclusive of the legs. A little bit of the skin of the back is just hung on the bend of the hook in such a manner that it does not hinder the free motion of the little chap; the more he tries to strike out and swim away, the more attractive it will prove. In using any of these baits, the bullet on the line should first of all be wound tight up against the top ring of the rod; only the bait and a foot of gut now hang from the rod point. An opening in the bushes can, I daresay, be found somewhere handy where this little line can be insinuated through. If not, turn the rod round and round until the gut hook is wound round it, and after poking it through a convenient hole, turn the rod the reverse way, and this will free it again. As soon as the line is free, let the reel gently turn round by itself until the bait hangs some two or three inches above the water. Now stop the reel by a pressure of the finger on the edge, and look carefully about for signs of any chub, because I have always found it the safest and surest plan to get sport when the fish were to be seen. As soon a you get the exact spot, move the rod point in that direction as carefully as possible, taking care not to knock or rustle the boughs any more than you can help, and drop the bait gently down; only let the insect itself, or the frog, touch the water; don't plump the bullet in, nor yet any of the gut. The bait, if lively, will try to swim away, or, in case it is a winged insect, spin and burr about on the surface, making tiny rings in the water. If any chub are about they may come and have a look at you, and occasionally take the bait; but my experience is that if, during a long day's 'dibbling,' you put the bait carefully over a full dozen shoals of them, some of them two or three times over, and succeed in getting half-a-dozen fair-sized fish, you may congratulate yourself on a bit of extra good luck. It will be found an advantage before offering the bait to the chub, to look for a hole close at hand and near to the water, through which the landing-net can be quietly insinuated, and if this landing-net has a long handle all the better; a chance may be found of playing a fish near to it, and a sudden scoop finishes the business. If a chub does happen to take a bait, don't be flurried and snatch it out of his mouth before he fairly gets hold of it; be as cool as you can when you see him rising. Hold the rod as quietly and as firmly as possible, and as soon as his jaws close fairly over the bait, and he makes a half-turn preparatory to swimming away, fix him with a gentle upward jerk, and if it is a big one, look out for squalls. Don't, on the other hand, wait too long before striking. The chub takes a bait of this character very quickly, and the moment you perceive he has got it fairly, strike. In playing a chub under these circumstances, where the character of the swim is such that even a run of three or four yards would be fatal to your chance of landing him, it is the best to hold on tight and chance it; the rod, line and tackle are strong, and if at the first jerk you lift his head out of the water, keep it there, if possible, and run him towards the landing-net before he fairly realises what is the matter; pick up the net with the left hand, run it under him as he flounders on the surface, and he is yours. This is rather a summary proceeding, hauling them out before they have a chance of even giving a single kick for liberty; but it is necessary if you want them, as a headlong dive of only six inches under the surface may result in broken tackle, a lost fish, and a swim utterly ruined, for that day at least. In some places it will be necessary to use only half the rod, or at most three lengths only, and for this a couple of stout india-rubber bands will be useful for the purpose of securing the reel to that portion of the rod that is required. Sometimes the only cover available behind which you can hide is a bunch of reeds or flags; crawl up to the water carefully behind these reeds, and perhaps you may see, as I have done more than once, a chub within two feet of your nose. A very short rod is now the best. This is why I recommend the indiarubber bands, so that the reel and running line can be shifted about where required. The one thing necessary in a 'dibbler' is extreme quiet and caution; step about as gingerly as possible, keep as far away as you nicely can from the edge of the water, take advantage of every bit of cover, and minutely examine the water in every direction for signs of fish before putting the rod over the stream. A reckless, impulsive fisherman, whose patience is likely to be utterly exhausted in less than an hour, will never make a 'dibbler.' One of the best surface chubbers that I ever knew was a postman. He discovered one day a small shoal of four chub under a bush in a cunning corner at the bottom of a private garden, and, as he expressed it, 'set his stall out to capture them.' Two hours every midday he was off duty, and for the greater portion of that time might have been found trying to wheedle those four chub into his basket. At the end of fourteen days he had succeeded in landing three of them, and thought he should manage to get the other one within the month if all went well. Now this was a case of patience and perseverance with a vengeance; but it is only a sample of what may be expected sometimes, if the angler makes up his mind to be a successful 'dibbler.'

Another plan of surface angling for chub is by fly-fishing proper; that is, casting an artificial fly or insect, or a dead natural one, on the streams and shallows in the more open parts of the river. This is a very interesting branch of sport, and one that a good many practical anglers are particularly fond of. Given a suitable stream, and a well-stocked one, there is no more delightful way of spending a warm summer's evening; at least this is my opinion. For this branch of angling a special outfit is required; the rod, line and tackle of the float-fisherman would not be a success by any means. In the first place the rod must be more limber, but still of some considerable strength; in fact, some anglers use a peel, or very light salmon rod. My old rod that has stood the battle and the breeze for some considerable time now, is a sort of combination. It has three joints of equal length, and is fifteen feet long when put up. It is built entirely of lancewood, with the exception of two feet at the butt-end, some lighter material being employed there. A fairly powerful rod is an absolute necessity for this work, as a great strain is put on it when lifting a heavy insect from the water at the end of a long line when making a fresh cast. Besides, it is a frequent occurrence to hook the fly into flags or twigs that grow above the haunts of the chub, and a strongish haul is necessary to tear it free; and again, a four-pounder takes a little persuasion when hooked to come out of his fortress of old roots. This weapon should be fitted up with steel snake rings throughout; the ferrules be strong, and well set up; and the winch fittings should grip the reel-plate tight and securely. I have a handle a foot long fitted to my rod, and when used instead of the five-foot butt makes it a single-handed one eleven feet long; this is somewhat heavier than the general run of trout fly-rods, but it is a very useful combination indeed for all that, and will throw a heavy bait, such as a frog or a cockchafer, with ease and precision. Sometimes the long rod may not be required, the stream or the boughs can be cast over with a shorter one; and here is where the little handle comes in. An ordinary brass or bronzed check fly reel will also be required, and two and a half inches in diameter will be found a very useful size. Forty yards of good waterproof fly-line is the next item, and this should be a size stouter than the ordinary trout fly-line. I always use a No. 4 'Standard' line, and find nothing to equal it for wear and casting power.

Extra fine gut is a mistake when used in chub casts. Some anglers, indeed, use a light salmon cast, but an ordinary stout gut line three yards long will be found all that is necessary. If this cast is made from very stout gut at one end, tapered down towards the fly to ordinary stout gut, it will be all the better for casting with. A good chub cast for fishing the boughs with frog or chafer should be capable of standing a dead pull of four pounds; I don't recommend anything lighter, and the colour can be the dark smoky blue recommended in bottom fishing. One of the very best early baits that can be thrown on a chub stream is a natural cockchafer, sometimes called in the Midlands a locust. These curious brown beetles can be seen on warm evenings from June to August flying about the tops of hedges, bushes or trees; sometimes in very large numbers; buzzing about over one particular bush like a swarm of bees. A few sweeps with a fine-meshed net, something like a butterfly collector's, will result in the capture of a supply of them. An old coffee tin, with a few small holes in the lid, will act as a capital receptacle for these baits. In baiting firmly on a long loop of gut; a twelve inch length of stout gut, doubled in the centre, so that the two ends are bound to the shank of the hook will do nicely. Hang this loop of gut in the eye of a very fine baiting needle, pass the point of the latter completely through the insect from the head to the tail; taking care that the needle goes right through the centre of the body; push the insect close up to the bends of the hook, so that the two points are looking upwards, clear above the chafer's head; the shank of the hook should be hid in the body of the bait, both hook points and barbs standing clear, as it were, above its back. Unless this is attended to carefully, a difficulty would be found in hooking the fish; the hard shell or covering of the chafer would hinder the hook from penetrating, unless the points stood out perfectly clear. The baited hook can very easily be joined to the main gut line by the two loops in the usual manner, that is, put one loop over the other, drop the chafer through the opposite one, and draw tight. Almost any sort of beetle can be used in much the same way, but hardly any of them possess the same attraction as the chafer. Beetles will stand a good deal of hard usage; they can be thrown about at the end of a long line, for some considerable time before flying to pieces; whereas a soft moth or bee would whip to atoms in three casts. In using chafers during the early summer, the shallow streams and open waters are the best places to try; the bait is thrown upstream and across, and allowed to flat down until it sweeps in a semicircle round to the bank on which the angler stands. As soon as it reaches the end of the cast, the bait is picked clean off, and thrown to the full length of the line behind the fisherman, and then projected forward again in the same manner as before. If there is no stream to speak of, and the place is a wide shallow, cast the bait out in all directions, working the rod point up and down in a gentle sink and draw movement, withdrawing the bait and making a fresh cast every few seconds. Very small frogs are used a little later on in the season when the chub have left the shallows and gone under the boughs; the same tackle that fished the chafer will do for the frog. Before sticking the baiting needle through the frog, it will be as well to kill it by a smart tap on the head. Run the needle right through it from the head to the stern, and bring it out between the hind legs; draw the gut through until the double hook rests on the top of the head. Tie the hind legs firmly to the gut at full length with a morsel of yellow silk, and cast it out like a fly under the boughs, or any other likely place, allowing it to float down stream; or else work with a sink and draw movement just under the surface.

Artificial chafers and beetles are now made and sold, some of them being remarkably life-like. These are used in the same manner as natural ones, but in the case of artificials a little addition is necessary. They generally have a mounting of a single hook firmly fixed under the belly; this hook should be filled with gentles and if you can thread seven or eight on all the better; it gives the insect a more natural appearance; makes it look as though it had met with an accident and got its insides squeezed out. In rivers that are much disturbed by boating, it is best to rise early in the morning if you want to catch chub on the fly. A companion who knows the boughs and the best spots, and can quietly row the boat at the proper distance from them, while you stand up in the bow and put the fly over the fish, is a comrade worth having. In years gone by stones of chub have been taken in a single day by a couple of anglers adopting this plan.

With regard to an artificial fly for chub, I have found the Zulu as good as any; this is a hackled fly without wings, black in colour, the body ribbed with gold twist, and finished off with a brilliant scarlet tag or tail. If this fly is dressed on a No. 8 hook, it will be found quite large enough, particularly if the water is very low and bright, and the season somewhat advanced, say August and September. During the earlier months of the year, the chub seemed to prefer a good mouthful, and if the fly was garnished with as many gentles as could possibly be crowded on the hook, why! it was all the better. Some odd times even a No. 8 hook was too big, the Zulu being all the more attractive if dressed on a hook no larger than a No. 10. Just at the dusk of evening, or, indeed, when it is impossible to see the fly yourself, chub are to be caught, and for this I recommend only one fly at a time to be used; to be correct, I prefer this at any time. The flies most in evidence for evening and night fishing are the Coachman, a dark-bodied fly with white wings; the Bustard, and the White Moth. These can be dressed rather larger than for day fishing, say on a No. 5 or 6 hook, with plenty of body and wing about them. Let the gut be very strong, so that you can haul the chub ashore very quickly. Playing a fish in the dark, when you are not certain of the surroundings, would, ten to one, result in disappointment, when a little prompt and energetic action would succeed.